THE WINE OF ASTONISHMENT

THE WINE OF ASTONISHMENT

by

William Sears

. . . thou hast made us to drink the wine of astonishment . . . That thy beloved may be delivered.
Psalms 60:1–5

GEORGE RONALD
OXFORD

GEORGE RONALD, *Publisher*
Oxford
www.grbooks.com

First published 1963
Sixth reprint 1991
Revised edition 2008

ISBN: 978-0-85398-521-1

A catalogue record for this book is available
from the British Library

Cover design: Steiner Graphics

Printed in Great Britain
by Cromwell Press, Trowbridge, Wiltshire

CONTENTS

A NOTE FROM THE PUBLISHER

Since its first publication 45 years ago in 1963, *The Wine of Astonishment* has always been popular. Reprinted many times, it has also been translated into several languages.

The original text is unchanged in this edition, except to update statistics showing the growth of the Bahá'í community. Also, where new authoritative translations have been made since 1963 of passages from the Bahá'í Writings, these replace the translations used by the author in the original edition.

As a clear and straightforward explanation from the Bahá'í Writings of many puzzling or controversial Christian doctrines such as the Trinity, baptism, resurrection, miracles and others, *The Wine of Astonishment* continues to hold its appeal to Christian and non-Christian seekers.

CHAPTER ONE

THE SEALS ARE OPENED

It was a strange luncheon. We were an odd assortment: a Jew, a Christian, a Muslim, and myself a Bahá'í.

We were seated in a little coffee-shop, looking down on the blue waters of the Mediterranean, on the very spot where Roman galleys had unloaded their passengers in the days of the Caesars. Greeks had anchored their ships here in the distant age of Pericles and Socrates. The Phoenicians had used the harbour before them.

As I raised the delicious cup of Turkish coffee to my lips, I could see the slender minaret of the mosque of 'Akká, Israel. It rose graceful and white against the cerulean blue sky. The walls of the great prison-fortress completely hid the graceful arches of the Crusaders' cathedral which lay buried beneath. The splattered, rust-reddened cannon-balls of Napoleon were still embedded in the stone walls of the fortress, a mute testimony to the failure of the Little Corporal to bend this ancient city to his will.

The hills of Galilee, the home of Christ, rose in a distant, purple mist. Across the white-capped bay of Haifa, Mount Carmel slept like a giant leopard, watching, one eye on the sea, and the other on the plain of Sharon. Temples had been raised on the slopes of this sacred mountain to the goddess of Sidon, Astarte, worshipped by Jezebel. Here Elijah slew the priests of Baal. The waters of the river Kishon, down which the bodies floated to the sea, still emptied into the bay.

Pythagoras, it is said, came to this mountain because of its sacred reputation. According to the Roman historian Tacitus, the

Emperor Vespasian also came here, to consult an oracle of God believed to dwell on the mountainside.

The caves of Elijah were now half-hidden by the gathering afternoon shadows. Sacred literature records that the angel Michael revealed the mystery of the *last days* and of the *time of the end* to Elijah on this same Mount Carmel.[1]

The legendary stories of salvation and slaughter which this sea, plain, valley, and mountain could tell, would fill a hundred volumes, each one an encyclopedia.

Conquerors and settlers had swept into this land one after another, in successive waves: Semites, Egyptians, Hittites, Phoenicians, Assyrians, Babylonians, Greeks, Persians, Romans, French, Turks, Germans, Hebrews, Arabs, and in this present day, peaceful visitors from all parts of the world. Gods of every description had risen and fallen here. This land had been held sacred and holy by multitudes down through the ages. It was now the home of four great world religions. Surely there was no better place to talk of God.

We were sitting in a coffee-shop in 'Akká, Israel, now called Accho after its ancient Hebrew name. The city was known as Ptolemais during the reign of the conquering Egyptian dynasty. It was known as St Jean d'Acre at the time of the Crusades. It was the 'Akká of the Turks. Less than a century ago it had "sunk to the level of a penal colony" for "murderers, highwaymen and robbers."

This was the scene of our discussion, a site in which God had been a burning issue since the earliest days of history.

"I would like to see a religion that would please everybody," the Christian said, "and there's slim hope of accomplishing that miracle."

"Miracles are out!" my Muslim friend objected.

"What I'm saying," the Christian continued, "is that we each have our own Prophet, or Messenger, and our own Book. What we need is a religion that would unite them and still please everyone. And there isn't a ghost of a chance of that happening."

"Ghosts are out!" It was the Muslim again.

The Jew objected. "But isn't that a promise of the sacred Scriptures? That there will one day be one universal Faith?"

2

The Christian nodded. "The day of the 'one fold and one shep-herd'. And don't tell me shepherds are out."

"Maybe not shepherds," the Muslim replied, "but I'm not so sure about the wise men."

"There aren't many wise men among us these days," I told the three of them, "or we wouldn't still be sitting around waiting for the day of the one fold and one shepherd."

The Jew was indignant. "You do not believe it is coming?"

"I believe in the one fold and the one shepherd," I told him, "but the day isn't *coming*, it's come – and gone."

"He's been sitting too long in the sun," my Christian friend explained to the others. "Let's move into the shade."

"It's not the sun that bothers me," I said. "It's you three. I tell you the Shepherd has already come to bring all the holy flocks together, and unite all the people."

The Jew cocked his head wisely. "Then where is the one fold? Not in this world, surely," he added, pointing to the *Jerusalem Post* with its headlines of warfare and disputes.

"Where," I asked him, "is the apple when the apple seed is planted? The fruit will come as a result of the planting of the seed. I tell you that the seed *has* been planted."

The Muslim was abrupt. "Never mind the parable," he said. "Who is the shepherd? Where is his flock? What is his Book?"

"Bahá'u'lláh is the shepherd," I answered. "The Bahá'ís are His flock, and His Book – He has written over a hundred volumes."

The Christian was sceptical. "If such a Faith already exists, why haven't I heard of it?"

"Why? Because your own Bible says: 'I will work a work in your days, which ye will not believe, though it be told you.'"[2]

"That's exactly the point," he said. "It *hasn't* been told to me. How can you believe in something you've never heard of?"

"You're hearing of it now," I told him. "Besides, your Book, your Bible, in the very next verse says that this will all take place at the *time of the end*. And then it adds that at that time '. . . the earth shall be filled with the knowledge of *the glory of the Lord*, as the waters cover the sea.'"[3]

When I explained that the name of the Founder of the Bahá'í Faith, Bahá'u'lláh, when translated into English means *the Glory of the Lord*, my Jewish friend shrugged.

"Well," he said "if his name *had* filled the earth, we *might* have heard of it."

"You think the Bahá'í Faith is not well known?"

"Is it?" he asked. "Who knows about it?"

"How about the people in eight thousand Bahá'í centres in over two hundred and fifty-seven countries, sovereignties, and dependencies in every part of the planet? People of every race, class, and previous religious conviction."

I could see that they were surprised, so I showed them a map which outlined the astonishing spread of the Bahá'í Faith during the last ten years.

"Look," I said. "Houses of Worship raised up in every continent, one of them called the first new thing in architecture since the thirteenth century."

"It's news to me."

"It shouldn't be," I said. "Bahá'u'lláh wrote to the kings and rulers of the world from this very city, Accho. He told them about the very things we've been discussing here today. He said that these truths were the foundations of all religious belief."

The Jew was intrigued. He asked me, "What are you doing in Israel? How did a television sports-broadcaster ever become interested in these subjects? You sound like a clergyman or a rabbi."

"By no means!" I laughed. "We have no paid clergy in the Bahá'í Faith. I'm here", I said, "on a visit to the World Centre of the Bahá'í Faith."

I won't recount the things I told them during the many hours and days we spent at that charming coffee-shop. We talked about God, life, and the future. I have related all these things in great detail in *Thief in the Night**, the book which I began writing seven

---

* *Thief in the Night* (George Ronald) tells the unique and fascinating story of the fulfillment of Scriptural prophecy, from all the sacred Books, as a proof of the validity of the Mission of Bahá'u'lláh, Founder of the Bahá'í Faith. This book is written from notes made before I accepted the Faith of Bahá'u'lláh. Therefore, it is written from a Christian viewpoint. Perhaps now, as a Bahá'í, I would write it differently; however the essential, basic story would remain unchanged, it would grow only in stature.

4

years ago as a detective story, and in which I submit a solution to *The Strange Case of the Missing Millennium.* In solving that century-old mystery of why Christ did not return as expected, I discovered the Bahá'í Faith and Bahá'u'lláh.

I shared with my new-found friends in 'Akká a brief list of proofs taken from one chapter of *Thief in the Night.*[4]

"Bahá'u'lláh", I assured them, "offers volumes of proofs that He is the One foretold in all the holy Books."

"*The Torah?*"

I nodded.

"*The New Testament?*"

"Yes."

"*The Qur'án?*"

"All three," I assured them. "And more. Bahá'u'lláh has also ful-filled the promises of the *Bhagavad-Gita,* the *Zend-Avesta,* as well as the hopes and dreams of the philosopher, the agnostic, and the skeptic."

With the exactness of the stars, and with an over-flowing abundance of proof, Bahá'u'lláh fulfilled prophecy after prophecy concerning the *Messiah who would appear in the last days* to bring about the day of the "one fold and one shepherd". I shared the fol-lowing few with my new-found friends:

1. Bahá'u'lláh's Faith appeared in the exact year foretold in the prophecies of *Daniel, Matthew, Luke, Revelation,* the *Qur'án,* and the ancient Jewish Scriptures.
2. He came to Israel as promised from the East.
3. Bahá'u'lláh came to Israel from ancient Assyria, from Persia as foretold.
4. He is known as "The Glory of God".
5. He came to the land of Canaan from the valley of the Tigris and Euphrates, as Abraham had come before Him.
6. He was descended from Abraham, to whose "seed" was prom-ised the land of Canaan in the last days.
7. Bahá'u'lláh came to Israel "by way of the sea".
8. He came, as promised in the astonishing prophecies of Micah,

from "fortified city to fortified city", from "the fortress to the river", from "mountain to mountain", and from "sea to sea".

9. Bahá'u'lláh's Faith has its World Centre on the side of Mount Carmel; so He feeds his flock, as promised, from "the midst of Carmel".

10. Carmel and Sharon have both seen Him, and have felt His presence, and He was known as "The Glory of the Lord" which they would behold.

11. His Law has "gone down from the mountain" to all parts of the world; from its world headquarters on Mount Carmel to Bahá'í communities in every part of the planet.

12. Surrounding the magnificent Shrines and administrative buildings of His Faith, the Bahá'í gardens on Mount Carmel and in the sandy plain of 'Akká have made the desert ". . . blossom as the rose".

13. The "place of his sanctuary" and His "rest" has been "beautified", as foreseen by Isaiah.

14. The place where Bahá'u'lláh's "feet" have walked has been made "glorious" with red and white paths, green lawns, flowering trees and blossoms of every description.

15. The children of Israel have been gathered together in His day; the Edict permitting them to return for the first time in twelve centuries to their homeland was signed in the very year, almost at the very moment, of the birth of His Faith.

16. A "house of prayer" for "all nations" will be raised on the side of the "mountain of God".

17. Bahá'u'lláh's ministry on earth lasted exactly "forty years" as foretold.

18. He "glorified" Christ and the greatness of Jesus throughout His writings.

19. He "toppled the kings" from their thrones, and had written to them first, foretelling their fate.

20. He has "unsealed" the holy Books of the past.

Each one of these proofs is supported by an entire chapter of intriguing details in *Thief in the Night*, a book which tells this amazing story in three hundred pages. The final two proofs (19) "He shall topple the kings from their thrones," and (20) "He shall unseal the Books," were so filled with entertainment and promise that I decided to devote an entire book to each of them.

The first of these books, *Fire in the Sky!**, tells the story of Bahá'u'lláh's Letters to the kings of the earth. The second book is this one, *The Wine of Astonishment.* In its own way, it is equally as dramatic and exciting as the others. I think you will agree, once you have read it, that Bahá'u'lláh leaves no doubt about the fact that He has "unsealed" the Books and revealed their hidden, inner meanings. As is the case with each story associated with the life of Bahá'u'lláh, the cup is not only "filled", it "runneth over".

This book gives Bahá'u'lláh's own explanations concerning those controversial subjects in the Bible which have troubled and confused mankind for centuries, and which have led to discord and separation among the followers of religion. We share with you in this volume the Writings of Bahá'u'lláh which will "unseal" the "hidden meanings" of such subjects as:

The end of the world
The Day of Judgment
Baptism
The Bread and Wine (Eucharist)
The Trinity
Confession and Penance
Good and Evil
The Son of God
The Father
Heaven and Hell (Purgatory and Limbo)
The Stars falling from Heaven
The darkening of the Sun and the Moon; the Moon turning to
    blood

---

* *Fire in the Sky!* The story of Bahá'u'lláh's Letters to the kings and rulers of His day, and the consequences of their disinterest, denial, and disobedience to the laws of love and justice which Bahá'u'lláh appealed to them to uphold. Published as *The Prisoner and the Kings* originally published by General Publishing Company Ltd, Toronto (1971) and reprinted by the Bahá'í Publishing Trust, Wilmette, IL (2007).

The Day of God
The Seal of the Prophets
The Return
The Resurrection

The ancient religious writings, in speaking of the Messiah at *the time of the end,* promise:

This is the Son of man ... who will reveal all the treasures of that which is concealed.[5]

The Old Testament foretells:

And in that day shall the deaf hear the words of the book, and the eyes of the blind shall see ... They also that erred in spirit shall come to understanding, and they that murmured shall learn doctrine.[6]

The New Testament promises the same:

... judge nothing before *the time, until the Lord come,* who ... will bring to light the *hidden things* of darkness ...[7]

This book, *The Wine of Astonishment,* has been written to demonstrate that Bahá'u'lláh has fulfilled all these promises. It offers proof that in His teachings you will find the wisdom, love, guidance, and assurance for which the peoples of all religions have been waiting for such a long, long time.

Is it any wonder that my friends were interested? They returned night after night to the coffee-shop to hear more about this true story of our own day which rivalled the thousand and one nights of Scheherazade.

I will now share with you the many things we spoke about during those magic twilights beside *Mare Nostrum,* the Roman sea.

CHAPTER TWO

OUT OF THE SEA OF KNOWLEDGE

I had planned to write *The Wine of Astonishment* in a leisurely fashion when next I returned to the Holy Land, but the immediate and surprisingly dramatic response to *Thief in the Night* forced an earlier deadline.

After neglecting to investigate the astonishing story of Bahá'u'lláh and the Bahá'í Faith for nearly a century, people in every part of the world now suddenly seem eager to inquire about Him. Interested seekers from all backgrounds want to know exactly what Bahá'u'lláh has written and taught about the Scriptures.

It was a blistering summer day when I finally settled down to work. I had eaten breakfast in Tel Aviv, "spring hill", and had lunched in Jaffa. I was thinking of the gods of other days as I gazed across the blue waters towards Cyprus. I could see Aphrodite rising from the foam of this ancient sea and wafting along the waves towards the mystic island. I thought of her counterpart in Sidon to the north, the enchanting Astarte.

This seaport of Jaffa was the Joppa of Jonah, and it was here, near where I sat, that he boarded the ill-fated vessel which carried him to his appointment with the whale. This was the neighbour-hood where Delilah was born, the Japho of the Philistines. It was even said by some to be the Jophey of mythology, and that out to sea was Andromeda's Rock, where the sacrificial maiden was bound to the stone, helplessly awaiting the sea-monster, until Perseus came to her rescue.

Here Peter raised Tabitha from the dead. As I thought about the meaning of this event, I began to write the book in my head.

I stopped off at Caesarea on the way back to Haifa. Ironically, I was walking beside a twentieth-century golf course when I made up my mind to make the two-thousand-year journey back to the days of Christ.

I could see the shore where St Paul had landed upon his return to Jerusalem after his great teaching victories in Ephesus. I was standing near the road along which Paul had been led to his imprisonment in the judgment hall of Herod, where he was held captive by the Roman governor, Felix.

The beach and adjacent land were littered with pottery and objects taken from the recent archeological diggings at this historic spot. Some accounts stated that an object had been uncovered with part of the name Pontius Pilate engraved upon it. Pilate had had a summer home along this same sea-washed shore. Peter had converted the Roman centurion here.

I walked along the seashore, thinking, "Perhaps on the very spot where I am standing, Peter and Paul stood." I thought of that other Caesarea, "the coasts of Caesarea Philippi", where Jesus had said of Peter's faith: "Upon this rock I will build my church." But this did not prevent His saying to this same Peter: "Get thee behind me, Satan."

What had He meant by these two greatly conflicting statements?

There, Christ had told His disciples that He "must go unto Jerusalem" to be slain and to rise from the dead.

What did this incredible statement really signify? There, Christ had promised that in *the last days* He would return "in the glory of the Father". What was the meaning of this?

In that same chapter of *Matthew,* which recounts the visit of Jesus to Caesarea Philippi, Christ spoke of the "sign of Jonah, the Prophet" who was three days and nights in the belly of the whale. He spoke of the "bread" that men should eat to be saved.

These brief fragments from His holy lips have crystallized into doctrines which have, over the centuries, confused readers of the Scriptures. They have caused new sects of Christ's Faith to arise, and have launched disputes, persecutions, and wars.

I decided to leave Caesarea at once and return to my rooms on the side of Mount Carmel, and to begin writing *The Wine of Astonishment*.

Bahá'u'lláh had so clearly and wonderfully explained the answers to these puzzling questions that it seemed almost tragic that the majority of mankind should still remain unaware of this remarkable story. Surely it was long past time that a humanity disillusioned with its present-day world should at last have the opportunity of tasting the "wine of astonishment" from the "new wine skins" of Bahá'u'lláh's teachings. I wanted all men to drink deeply and be refreshed.

As shown more fully in *Thief in the Night* (pp. 47–52), it was not possible, according to both the Old and New Testaments, for anyone to understand thoroughly the meaning of the words of the Scriptures until the present day. According to prophecy, the Books had been "sealed" until *the time of the end*. For example:

In *Isaiah, Daniel,* and *Revelation*, a remarkable series of prophecies point out that (1) the Book of Scripture is sealed, and that (2) *in the last days* the Book will be opened. *Isaiah* in one chapter says:

1. *Sealed:* "And the vision of all is become unto you as the words of a book that is *sealed*, which men deliver to one that is learned, saying, Read this, I pray thee: and he saith, I cannot; for *it is sealed:*"[1]

2. *Unsealed:* "And *in that day* shall the deaf hear the words of the book, and the eyes of the blind shall see ... They also that erred in spirit shall come to understanding, and they that murmured shall learn doctrine."[2]

Isaiah continues his praise of the Holy One of Israel who will work these wonders in the last day. Finally, in a burst of praise, he says in a following chapter:

> ... the desert shall rejoice, and blossom as the rose ... the excellency of Carmel and Sharon, they shall see *the glory of the Lord. . .*[3]

It was from the "midst of Carmel" that Bahá'u'lláh revealed many of His most important teachings which helped "unseal" the Books. His name, in English, means *the Glory of the Lord,* or *the Glory of God.* Next, *Daniel:*

1. *Sealed:* "Go thy way, Daniel: for the words are closed up and *sealed* till *the time of the end.*"[4]
2. *Unsealed:* "I beheld till the [other] thrones were cast down, and the Ancient of days did sit ... and ten thousand times ten thousand stood before him: the judgment was set, and *the books were opened.*"[5]

This last promise of the "unsealing" is given by *Daniel* in the same chapter in which he says that "one like the Son of man came with the clouds of heaven". The very words Christ Himself used for His own return, saying: "I will come in the clouds of heaven."

Revelation ends all doubt on this subject. The basic theme of this entire Book is the *second* coming of Christ. *Revelation* states plainly that those books which were sealed until *the time of the end* of Christ's return, would then be opened, and would be sealed no more:

Seal *not* the sayings of the prophecy of this book; for *the time is at hand.*[6]

Then *Revelation,* like *Daniel,* repeats the same vision of the coming of the Messiah, the return of Christ. *Daniel* uses the same description as Christ Himself for that day when the books would be unsealed:

And I looked, and behold a white cloud, and upon the cloud one sat like unto the Son of man ...[7]

Revelation says of this Lamb of God, who will appear in the last days:

Thou art worthy to take the book, and *to open the seals* thereof
. . .[8]

Revelation also says of this Lamb that he was the light of the city of God, the New Jerusalem which was the Word of God. In the same verse, this Book says of this day:

. . . *the glory of God* did lighten it. . .[9]

Now let us examine the teachings of the Faith of Bahá'u'lláh, whose name means *the Glory of God*. Let us test Him, and see if He has proved Himself "worthy to open the seals" of the sacred Scriptures. Let us look for convincing proof that He has honestly unsealed "the wine of astonishment" so that a troubled world "may be delivered". For if He *has* "unsealed" the meaning of the sacred Scriptures, He is the hope of the world; and His teachings may well be the sole means for rescuing our civilization from self-destruction.

CHAPTER THREE

HOW TO UNRAVEL THE SECRET OF THE SCRIPTURES

The famous scholar, Charles Baudouin, in his *Contemporary Studies,* writes glowingly of the explanations to be found in the teachings of Bahá'u'lláh. He says they are "permeated with a sane and noble mysticism; . . . nothing could speak more intimately to the soul, in low tones, and as if from within . . . such is the new dawn in the East. We should give them our close attention; we should abandon our customary mood of disdainful superiority . . . [Bahá'u'lláh's] ethical code is dominated by the law of love taught by Jesus and by all the Prophets. In the thousand and one details of practical life, this law is subject to manifold interpretations. That of Bahá'u'lláh is unquestionably one of the most comprehensive of these, one of the most exalted, one of the most satisfactory to the modern mind . . ."[1]

Bahá'u'lláh, in His teachings, has given us the key with which to unlock the "hidden meanings" of the Bible as well as of the other Holy Books. In order to understand these holy Writings, it is imperative that we grasp the following basic truth:

Human knowledge is of two kinds. One is the knowledge of the senses: sight, hearing, touch, taste, and smell. We have a knowledge of many things through these outer senses. For example: the sun can be seen by the eye; sounds can be heard by the ear; heat and cold can be felt by the touch; foods can be tasted; perfumes can be perceived by the sense of smell. These things are all apparent to the outer, physical senses. This is the first kind of knowledge.[2]

The second kind of human knowledge is intellectual.

Intellectual realities are not perceptible to the senses. They have no outward form. They occupy no space. They cannot be seen, heard, touched, tasted, or smelled. Love is such a reality. The ear cannot hear love, nor can the eye see it. Love cannot be touched, tasted, or perceived by the sense of smell. Joy is also an intellectual reality of this nature. Knowledge, likewise, cannot be recognized by the outward senses. These are not material things. They are intellectual or spiritual qualities.

The Writings of Bahá'u'lláh's Faith point out that in order to explain these inward *intellectual* or *spiritual* realities, it is necessary to use figures or symbols which are apparent to the outward senses. This is the easiest and most effective way in which such spiritual truths can be understood. Sometimes it is the only way.

For example: if you wish to prove to others that you are happy, it isn't enough simply to say, "I am happy." This statement alone cannot prove you are happy. It cannot convey your inner feeling in the manner you wish. Therefore, you use an *outward* symbol to express this *inward* feeling. You say, "My heart is singing like a lark!"; or, "My heart is soaring in the skies like a cloud!"; or, "I am so happy that it is springtime in my heart."

If you are in deep sorrow or grief, you say, "My heart is heavy"; or, "I am filled with black despair." You use things that are apparent to your listeners' *outward* senses in order to convey your *inward* spiritual condition. Only in this way can others clearly understand your feelings and thoughts.

The best example is perhaps this one. Man has used *light* as a symbol of knowledge, and *darkness* as a symbol of ignorance for centuries. When a man understands something, he says, "I see the light." When a problem is difficult to solve, he says, "Who can shed some light (meaning knowledge) upon this difficulty?" We speak of primitive tribes living in the "darkness of ignorance". We say that cruel people are in the "darkness of error".

Yet knowledge is not a light which is apparent to the outward sense of sight. Nor are ignorance and error outwardly visible as darkness. Light and darkness in this sense are used as symbols.

15

We say symbolically that the earth has succumbed to winter and is *dead;* but soon the spring will come and *revive* it. We say that one who is inattentive is *asleep.* We say that one who does not grasp things quickly is a "dead-head". One who misses a meaning, we say, "is asleep at the switch". We call one who is cruel a *tiger,* one who is sly a *snake,* one who is wise an *owl,* and one who is vicious a *mad dog.* These are all outward symbols which are used to reveal an inward characteristic, truth, or reality.

When we seek to explain the intellectual or spiritual realities, we are obliged to express them in a form which the outward senses can comprehend. Until the student of Scriptures understands this fundamental truth, the holy Books will remain incomprehensible to him. They seem contrary to reason. They are "sealed up" and closed to him. But once this truth is recognized, the unity and beauty to be found in the meanings of the sacred Scriptures immediately become apparent. What previously divided men, now unites them. What was impossible for the logical mind to accept before, now becomes something lucid and inspiring.[3]

The people in the time of Christ did not understand this basic truth. Hence they denied Him. They could not accept Christ as the one promised by Moses. Moses had used outward symbols to indicate inward truths concerning the coming of the Messiah. The Old Testament was filled with such symbols, but the followers of Moses forgot that these outward symbols represented inward truths. They clung to the symbol itself, forgetting the inward meaning. Hence, in the day when Christ appeared, they denied Him and His Message, as the following demonstrates.

Their holy Book said that the Messiah would come from an unknown place, would rule by a sword, would sit upon the throne of David, would promulgate the law of Moses.

"Christ", they said, "has done none of these things. Therefore, He is obviously an imposter. He came from Nazareth, which is only too well known. He had no sword, nor an army by which to rule. He had no throne to sit upon. In fact, he didn't even have a carpet to lie upon. He not only failed to promulgate and establish the law of Moses, he openly violated it."

These people clung to the outward symbol rather than the inward truth. For, inwardly, each of these promises *was* fulfilled.

(1) Christ came from the womb of Mary, but His spirit came from God, from heaven, a place unknown to men. (2) The sword by which He ruled was the sword of His tongue. (3) The blade of His teachings cut through the enemy of opposition and divided believer from non-believer. (4) His throne was in the hearts of men. (5) History has shown that He did indeed promulgate and establish the law of Moses. However, not as the people of His day had expected. Wherever the Christian Bible is read today, it contains not only the New Testament of Christ, but also the Old Testament of Moses. Thus, the Law of the great "Interlocutor" has been carried into all parts of the planet and "promulgated" by the Mission of Christ.

Bahá'u'lláh wrote an entire volume, over two hundred and fifty pages in length, in which He carefully explains these hidden scriptural meanings which have for such a long time confused the people of religion.

This *Book of Certitude* written by Bahá'u'lláh is a source and reference book for the scholar and student.*

Bahá'u'lláh has written of these explanations:

This is the Day whereon human ears have been privileged to hear what He Who conversed with God [Moses] heard upon Sinai, what He Who is the Friend of God [Muhammad] heard when lifted up towards Him, what He Who is the Spirit of God [Jesus] heard as He ascended unto Him, the Help in Peril, the Self-Subsisting.[4]

With the aid of this "sea of knowledge", we shall examine certain specific instances in which the people of the past have clung to the *outward* symbol of Scripture, neglecting the *inward* truth; thus they were misled into error. The explanations offered here are

---

* *Kitáb-i-Íqan* (Book of Certitude). Also read *Some Answered Questions*, written by 'Abdu'l-Bahá, the son of Bahá'u'lláh; this book also gives penetrating answers to those questions most commonly asked by Christians.

the explanations which have been given by Bahá'u'lláh Himself. They are not explanations which His followers arrived at long after His own time. Here you will find the answers which Bahá'u'lláh Himself, with His own pen, has given to these age-old questions.

Bahá'u'lláh, as shown in *Thief in the Night,* has offered the world overwhelming proof of the truth of His Mission. Now, we shall examine additional proof. We shall test the meanings which He has *unsealed* from those Books which *Isaiah, Daniel,* and the New Testament say were "sealed up" until "the time of the end".

Bahá'u'lláh has given the following promise:

This is the sealed and mystic Scroll, the repository of God's irrevocable Decree ... that lay wrapt within the veil of impenetrable mystery, and hath now been sent down as a token of the grace of Him Who is the Almighty ... In it have We ... written down the knowledge of all things from first to last.[5]

CHAPTER FOUR

THE MEANING BEHIND THE RITUAL OF BAPTISM

A recent article in a national magazine pointed out the extremes to which mankind has gone with regard to what was once a simple, beautiful truth. A minority of the "Do Good" Baptists disagreed with the doctrine of the group, the article alleged, and moved down the river to start a new church called the "Do Better" Baptists.

The ritual of baptism has caused almost as many disputes and divisions within the Christian ranks as have the differences of opinion regarding the Trinity. The forms and rituals of baptism have become multiplied, varied and impressive. Many church members have unwittingly replaced their belief in the inward truth of baptism with an acceptance of the outward form. Thus, the meaning of baptism as taught by Christ has been lost. The symbol has replaced the *inward truth*. The true significance of baptism has vanished in a maze of man-made and often conflicting rituals.

In order to restore a spirit of unity, Bahá'u'lláh's teachings have explained once again the inner significance of baptism. It is this: as the body becomes purified and wholesome through the use of water to cleanse it, in like manner the soul of man becomes cleansed and freed from impurities when bathed in the spirit of belief in God.

The meaning of baptism can be expressed in these words: "Oh God! As my body is washed free of physical blemishes by this water, in the same way cleanse and sanctify my soul from the impure things which are not worthy of Thy presence."

True baptism is not with material water. It is with symbolical water – the water of knowledge and belief in God.

If a man's heart is impure, if he hates his fellow men, he can wash his body with material water forever, and will still not be cleansed within. Baptism with water is an *outward symbol* of an *inward truth*. It is the act of being purified of one's past errors by the water of the knowledge of God, as given to mankind by His Messenger.

Throughout the Holy Books this symbol of water is used to represent knowledge. In Jeremiah, the Lord says:

> My people ... have forsaken me the fountain of living waters ...[1]

Revelation speaks of the Lamb who will "unseal" the books in *the last days*, and says that this Lamb will:

> ... lead them unto living fountains of waters.[2]

Isaiah also uses this symbol of water for knowledge; and speaks as well of its use in *the last days*, saying:

> And the Lord shall guide thee continually, and satisfy thy soul in drought ... and thou shalt be like a watered garden ...[3]

This particular passage is especially interesting, in view of the fact that Bahá'u'lláh's name, when translated into English, means the Glory of the Lord. For, in this very same chapter, Isaiah promises:

> ... *the glory of the Lord* shall be thy rereward ... thou shalt cry, and he shall say, Here I am.[4]

Of all the Old Testament prophets, perhaps Habakkuk uses most effectively and clearly the symbol of water to represent the knowledge of God. He declares in a prophecy mentioned earlier:

> For the earth shall be filled with the knowledge of *the glory of the Lord*, as the *waters* cover the sea.[5]

And once again we see the promise of *the glory of the Lord* (Bahá'u'lláh) who will bring this "water" of life. Habakkuk carefully points out that it will take inward vision to understand this truth, for he says:

> ... regard, and wonder marvellously: for I will work a work in your days, which *ye will not believe, though it be told you.*[6]

Christ also used this same symbol of *water* in speaking to the people of His day. He said:

> Except a man be born of water and of the Spirit, he cannot enter into the kingdom of God.[7]

Obviously a man cannot be born physically of material water. However, he *can* be born spiritually by drinking the water of the knowledge of God, and by believing in God's Messenger, Who offers it. Christ made the symbology even more unmistakable saying:

> Except a man be born again, he cannot see the kingdom of God.[8]

Man must be born *again* of this water of life. In other words, he must believe. The people in the time of Christ thought that He (Jesus) was talking utter nonsense when He told them they must be born again.

"What does the Nazarene mean?" they asked. "Is it possible for a man to return to his mother's womb full-grown, that he might be born again? This teaching is nonsense."

From their limited understanding, they were of course right. To the outward senses this was both impossible and unreasonable. But Christ's words were symbolic, not literal.

Belief in the Messenger of God and acceptance of His Word is the true baptism in every age in which a Messenger of God appears. This baptism (rebirth) obviously requires that the person being baptized be old enough to understand what he is being taught. Each person must decide for himself whether or not he believes, before being baptized. The practice of baptizing children and infants, who were too young to participate in the ceremony with their own minds, was not a part of Christ's teaching. It was introduced into the Christian church long after the time of Christ.

Bishop Barnes writes: ". . . it is hardly necessary to say that there is no evidence for infant baptism in the early church." He then quotes the Church fathers who speak of fasting as being necessary before baptism, and being used as a regular practice. "One may doubt", he adds, "if any mother would let her infant fast 'one or two days before': a fast of even a few hours would be impractical."[9]

When the Church adopted the doctrine of original sin, classifying every human being born into the world as being born with the sin of Adam and Eve upon his soul, it became necessary to baptize infants as well as adults. Only in this way could the stigma be removed. For centuries there was considerable feeling that since a boy child born into the Jewish Faith must be circumcized within eight days of his birth, so each Christian child should be baptized in Christ as soon as possible after his or her birth, preferably within eight days.

The church of the East and the church of the West differed in their views. Not only in the matter of baptism, but in almost every item of church service. Their constant disputes clearly indicated that these were matters, not of basic belief but rather of human interpretation.

It has been said that the Eastern Church or Greek Church, and the Western Church or Latin Church, were "like a biological species divided in space and diversified in time".[10]

Their differences grew with the passing of time until eventually the Roman Church baptized by aspersion (sprinkling), and the Greek Church by immersion. The Greek Cross had arms of equal length, while the Latin Cross was elongated. Furthermore, the "Greeks prayed standing, the Latins kneeling ... marriage was forbidden to Latin, permitted to Greek, priests; Latin priests shaved, Greek priests had contemplative beards. The Latin clergy specialized in politics, the Greek in theology," and so on.[11]

In both the Greek and Roman churches the idea of belief in Christ *before* baptism gradually was lost. Godparents assumed the *thinking* and *believing* role for the infant. When Charlemagne began his great Christianizing campaign, he as king did the thinking for his would-be converts. He gave the Saxons he conquered a choice: be baptized or be slain. In one day he beheaded 4,500 Saxons.

Baptism removed all past sins, but made no provision for future sins. Thus, for centuries, the danger of sinning after baptism was considered so serious that many Christians postponed their baptism until their deathbeds, the Emperor Constantine being perhaps the most famous example. This practice of postponing baptism was perilous, in that a believer might die unbaptized. It was also ruinous to the Church as it tacitly permitted sin.

At length, one sin after baptism was permitted. This opened the door, and gradually more sins were permitted. A Christian clergyman writes, ". . . in the end the ecclesiastical discipline of confession and absolution became standardized."[12]

Thus, it became possible to sin after baptism and still be saved through confession, absolution, and communion.

The New Testament proves beyond doubt that it was necessary for the people to *understand* the Words of Christ and to *believe* in Him before being baptized. The words of the Gospels and of the Acts of the Apostles assure us that there is no true baptism where the mind does not participate in this rebirth. It is indeed, as Bahá'u'lláh explains, *the water of knowledge* that is used. Christ demonstrated this truth when He said:

He that *believeth* and is baptized shall be saved . . .[13]

It was necessary to *believe* first, then to be baptized. In another place, Christ says:

Go ye therefore, and *teach* all nations, baptizing them in the name of the Father, and of the Son, and of the Holy Ghost.[14]

23

It is plain that the people must first be *taught*. When they understand and believe, then they are baptized. The baptism is merely the *outward* fulfilment of this inward belief. Paul understood this principle, and said:

> Christ sent me not to *baptize*, but to *preach* the gospel ...[15]

Paul knew that belief in Christ was the important thing. Once this belief existed, the baptism of the spirit was accomplished, but such baptism was always secondary to belief. For example, it is written in *Acts*:

> and many of the Corinthians hearing *believed*, and were *baptized*.[16]

Peter also understood this symbolic truth. It is said of him:

> Then Peter said unto them, *Repent*, and be *baptized* ...[17]

It required from the people an act of the will to repent. They must give up the old ways and concepts and accept the new belief. Then they could be baptized.

Three verses later comes yet another example of, first, the *belief* and then, second, the *baptism*:

> Then they that gladly *received his word* were *baptized*: ...[18]

There are these additional clear references:

> But when they *believed*... the things concerning the kingdom of God ... they were *baptized* ...[19]

> Then Simon himself *believed* ... and ... he was *baptized* ...[20]

There is evidence that more than a century after Christ, this *believing* still preceded baptism. Justin Martyr, in his *First Apology* in the chapter on worship, wrote that those "who are persuaded and believe that what we teach them and say is true, and undertake to live accordingly, are instructed to pray and to exhort God with fasting for the remission of their past sins" before being baptized.

The *Shepherd of Hermas* proposed that "The righteous dead need the preaching of the gospel and also baptism that they may be saved." Barnes,[21] in speaking of this book which hovered so long on the edge of the New Testament, says, "Though Hermas thus associates preaching with baptism, it seems not unfair to say that he attaches to the rite a magical significance. Those who are baptized 'descend into the water dead, and they rise alive.'"[22]

And a final proof from the New Testament which shows conclusively that water alone is useless unless accompanied by belief:

> And as they went on their way, they came unto a certain water: and the eunuch said, See, *here is water*; what doth hinder me to be baptized?
>
> And Philip said, *If thou believest with all thine heart*, thou mayest. And he answered and said, *I believe* ... and he *baptized* him.[23]

Belief is the important thing. Christ, in another place, said that "*Whosoever believeth*" in Him should not perish, but would have "*eternal life*". Therefore, it was obviously possible to have this eternal life and be saved without the baptism with material water. Jesus said to the thief on the cross:

> Today shalt thou be with me in paradise.[24]

The thief believed, and without the baptism of material water, he gained eternal life. Another similar case is recorded:

> And he [Jesus] said to the woman, *Thy faith hath saved thee*; go in peace.[25]

No material water was needed for her salvation. Unquestionable proof that material water is not necessary for baptism, other than as a symbol, is found in *Luke*, where it says of Jesus:

... he shall baptize you with the Holy Ghost and with fire:[26]

No one would desire to be baptized by immersion in flames, or by sprinkling with physical fire, for obvious reasons. The fire spoken of here is the "fire of the love of God" which burns away our impurities and helps us to believe.

The Greek word from which baptism is derived means both "to dip" and "to purify". The former is but the symbol which conveys the inward truth of the latter. Unfortunately, the outward symbol has been given such importance in itself that a great many people have completely forgotten the inward reality which it represents. They have lost sight of the sincere belief and inner decision which gives baptism its original meaning and life. Many are baptized who don't believe with all their hearts and souls. Many don't believe at all. It has become merely a form. Gradually, every form of baptism imaginable developed: *private baptism*; *baptism by desire* which requires nothing more than the dying wish; *baptism for the dead*, so that the living might be baptized on behalf of non-Christians no longer living; *baptism by proxy* in which, in singular cases, one person can be baptized for as many as fifty other souls who have died in original sin.

Baptism, of course, did not originate with Christianity. It was practised by John the Baptist, by the Essenes, and by the pagans of old. This process of cleansing also formed a part of the ritual of the Jews, long before the time of Christ. These Jewish "lustrations" were designed to "cleanse the body of ritual pollution", but were used on "various occasions, not once". Rowley writes, "Nevertheless, it is probable that Jewish lustrations have some historical connection with Christian baptism to the extent that the form of the ceremony developed out of the form of the lustrations." The Jews also practised proselyte baptism which "marked the experience of conversion from paganism to Judaism".[27]

Obviously, the ritual of baptism itself is without meaning unless the truth that lies behind the ritual is understood. Christ warned of the danger of professing belief with the outward sense of speech while disbelieving in the inward heart. He said:

> Not everyone that saith unto me, Lord, Lord, shall enter into the kingdom of heaven; but he that doeth the will of my Father which is in heaven.[28]

In every religion there is an *outward* form of demonstrating this *inward* belief in the Messenger of God, and of thus being accepted into His Faith. In Christianity it is baptism. In the Bahá'í Faith it is a simple declaration of belief. The purpose of each of these acts is identical. Each is a sign of rebirth, renewal, purification, and acceptance of the Messenger of God.

The method and name of the "expression of belief" changes from age to age, but the purpose is identical. Yet, as history clearly demonstrates, in each age the followers of the old Faith always deny the new. They cling tenaciously to their own ancient, exclusive, outward symbol, unaware that its inward spirit is dead.

A vast number of Christians in this day feel that only through baptism can a man be saved. In the day of Christ's early teaching many believed likewise that only through their own outward symbol, circumcision, the sign of the covenant with God, could they be faithful, and be saved. According to the injunction given in the Book of Genesis, each boy was to be circumcized. This was considered absolutely essential.

The custom of circumcision was not specialized to the Jews. It was also prevalent among the Egyptians, Ethiopians, Phoenicians, Arabs, and Syrians as a health measure and for reducing sexual excitability.

There is always the tendency of the followers of the new Faith to cling to the time-honoured customs of the old; not as a health measure, but as a symbol of the Covenant. Circumcision and baptism were clearly two different rites. Yet, many early Christians felt that baptism, like circumcision, should take place by the eighth day after birth. It is almost impossible for a new Faith to break away cleanly from the long-used rituals of its parent religion. The first fifteen Bishops of the Christian Church in Jerusalem were circumcized Jews. The ritual of circumcision, in its purely religious sense as a sign of the Covenant, had a powerful hold on their emotions.

The New Testament speaks of early Christian teachers, saying:

> . . . certain men which came down from Judea taught the brethren, and said, Except ye be circumcized after the manner of Moses, ye cannot be saved.[29]

Yet, the New Testament makes it clear that just as baptism is symbolical, so is circumcision. It is the belief that gives life, not the ritual. For example:

> Is any man called [to God] being circumcized? let him not become uncircumcized. Is any called in uncircumcision? let him not be circumcized.
>
> Circumcision is nothing, and uncircumcision is nothing, but the keeping of the commandments of God.[30]

The simple fact is this, Bahá'u'lláh tells us: the new Prophet comes with the same, eternal Faith brought by His Predecessor. He renews men's belief in the *inward* realities. He helps them to shake off the *outward* symbols which have become encrusted and meaningless. Habit, superstition and time have killed the spirit and hidden the true inner meaning of baptism. In its place the outward sign of water has now become the important thing. The conscience and spirit which prompted baptism in the beginning are lost entirely. The truth dies away at last, and men and children permit themselves to be baptized whether they have the inner belief or not. It is the conventional thing to do. It is the habit of their society.

The Apostle Paul called upon those whom he taught, urging them to see that circumcision was inwardly a spiritual thing. It was a way of expressing detachment from the world. Paul said:

. . . ye are circumcized with the circumcision made without
hands . . .[31]

Physically, of course, this was impossible, as impossible as being
baptized in fire. It was a circumcision of the spirit. It was a cutting
away of man's heart from the desires of the world. Bahá'u'lláh tells
us that in this day there is no longer a need for using an outer
symbol for this truth. The inner reality itself can now be clearly
understood by mankind.

The Books have been "unsealed" and their inner meanings
have been made clear. In this day, a man can read, study, and make
up his own mind. He can decide for himself when he is ready to
declare his inner decision or belief. It need no longer be done for
him by ritual, by proxy, or by the use of an outward symbol, water.
This is a new day, and mankind can now be baptized in a new
sense. Humanity can be cleansed (baptized) with the water of the
knowledge of God, and the fire of the love of God. The full beauty
and majesty of such a baptism can be found in the words and
teachings of God's Messenger for this age, Bahá'u'lláh, *the Glory
of God.*

Bahá'u'lláh writes:

Great indeed is this Day! The allusions made to it in all the
sacred Scriptures as the Day of God attest its greatness. The
soul of every Prophet of God, of every Divine Messenger, hath
thirsted for this wondrous Day. All the divers kindreds of the
earth have, likewise, yearned to attain it.[32]

CHAPTER FIVE

THE BREAD AND THE WINE, CONFESSION AND PENANCE

Let us examine another example in which entire groups of people have clung to the outward symbol, forgetting the inward truth; thus being led into grave errors that have lasted for centuries.

This is the symbol of *the bread and the wine.*

Christian sects and church groups have not only disagreed as to the inner meaning of this symbol, they have no common name for the sacrament itself. H. H. Rowley, in *The Unity of the Bible,* writes: "There is no agreement even as to the name by which it is known. To some it is the Lord's Supper, to others Holy Communion, to others the Eucharist, and to others the Mass:"[1]

Jesus said:

I am the living bread which came down from heaven: if any man eat of this bread, he shall live for ever: and the bread that I will give is my flesh, which I will give for the life of the world.[2]

In the same chapter, He adds:

Whoso eateth my flesh, and drinketh my blood, hath eternal life; and I will raise him up at the last day.[3]

"What manner of madness is this?" the people of Christ's day asked each other. "How is it possible to eat of his flesh? Who can believe in such a man?"

30

The Writings of the Bahá'í Faith help us to understand the meaning and beauty of these statements of Christ.

This *bread* signifies the heavenly food to be found in the teachings of Christ. "If any man eat of this bread" simply means that if any man believes in Christ, accepts Him, and lives according to His teachings, he will gain everlasting life. "Whoso drinketh my blood" has the same meaning. Just as physical food nourishes the body, so does the spiritual food, the words of Christ, nourish the soul of man. Just as the various members of the physical body gain vitality and sustenance from the blood, so does the spirit of man receive sustenance from these heavenly teachings.

Christ showed plainly that by "heavenly bread" He meant the spirit of His teachings. He declared:

It is the *spirit* that quickeneth; the *flesh* profiteth nothing . . . [4]

The *flesh* which man must eat, and which Christ speaks of in the previous verse, is the body of His teachings. This is the flesh that feeds mankind.

It was the same food that was given to mankind in the day of Moses. The same symbol was used concerning Moses and those followers who:

. . . were all baptized unto Moses in the cloud and in the sea;
And did all *eat* the same *spiritual meat*;[5]

This symbol is used again in another verse of *John* where it is written:

And Jesus said unto them, I am the bread of life: he that cometh to me shall never hunger; and he that believeth on me shall never thirst.[6]

Thus Christ expresses "coming to him" as *eating*; and "believing in him" as *drinking*. To *eat* is to draw near to Him, and to *drink* is to believe in Him. Whoever found guidance through the words of

Christ by approaching and believing in Him, had indeed partaken of the "last supper" of bread and wine; and thus they became numbered among the *living*. Whoever remained afar and disbelieved was without spiritual food, and was among the *dead*.[7]

In still another place, Christ referred to this drink in words which conclusively show its symbolic nature:

> Jesus stood and cried, saying, If any man thirst, let him come unto me, and drink.
>
> He that *believeth* on me, as the scripture hath said, out of his belly shall flow rivers of living water.[8]

The next verse says:

> But this spake he of the Spirit, which they that believe on him should receive ...[9]

Christ gave the same lessons privately to His disciples. He showed them that the "meat" of which He spoke was the teachings which God had given Him to deliver to mankind. It is recorded of Jesus:

> In the mean while his disciples prayed him, saying, Master, eat.
>
> But he said unto them, I have meat to eat that ye know not of.
>
> Therefore said the disciples one to another, Hath any man brought him aught to eat?
>
> Jesus saith unto them, *My meat* is to do the will of him that sent me, and to finish his *work*.[10]

The *meat* and the *bread* and the *wine* were all symbolical. They were inner nourishment described by an outward name. If the *bread and wine* were to have a purely physical meaning, they would be but a mere replica of many similar ceremonies held to honour the pagan gods of the past.

Cicero speaks of the *corn of Ceres* and the *wine of Bacchus*. Ritual cakes and grain were eaten in the worship of Osiris, and were identified with his *body*. They were said to possess mystic powers. Demeter and Dionysius were worshipped in a form of eucharistic ritual. The same is true of Attis.

A much closer parallel can be found in the cult of Mithra with its sacramental meal. Renan and Sir James Frazer both speak of it in their works. Durant writes, "In the mysteries of Mithras the worshippers were offered consecrated bread and water." He adds that the Spanish conquistadores were shocked to find similar rites "of a form of the sacred meal among the Indians of Mexico and Peru".[11]

We read that in the early days of the Church, "members of the congregation, especially women, were allowed to 'prophesy' – i.e. to 'speak forth' in a trance of ecstasy.... When these performances conduced to ritual fever and theological chaos, the Church discouraged and finally suppressed them."[12] These weekly ceremonies gradually developed into the Mass, but not until approximately two hundred years after Christ.

In fairness to the early Church, it must be pointed out that the Church did not deliberately set out to imitate pagan rites and superstitions. It had its hands full trying to control the flock, and to keep from being swamped by pagan ideas. The dilemma of the early Church arose partly from a misunderstanding of the meaning of Christ's words, and partly from a compromise made with pagan ideas in order to win popularity among the masses of people.

The Christian form of worship was too simple to impress either the Greek or the Roman. The pagans felt it was atheism because it had no images. The absence of priests proved to the pagans that there was no dignity in the Christian worship. Furthermore, the pagans felt that there could be no legal authority if there were no "sacrifices".

Near the end of the second century, priests and rites were added to Christian worship. In spite of its persecution of the Christians, the State ultimately was favourably impressed. Christian saints and images gradually replaced the multitudinous gods of everyday pagan life. Sacrifice came with the sacred meal as offered by the priest.

Durant states: "By the close of the second century these weekly ceremonies had taken the form of the Christian Mass. Based partly on the Judaic Temple services, partly on Greek mystery rituals of purification, vicarious sacrifice, and participation through communion, in the death-overcoming powers of the deity, the Mass grew slowly into a rich congerie of prayers, psalms, readings, sermons, antiphonal recitations, and, above all, that symbolic atoning sacrifice of the 'Lamb of God' which replaced, in Christianity, the bloody offerings of older faiths. The bread and wine, which these cults had considered as gifts placed upon the altar before the god, were now conceived as changed by the priestly act of consecration into the body and blood of Christ, and were presented to God as a repetition of the self-immolation of Jesus on the Cross. Then, in an intense and moving ceremony, the worshippers partook of the very substance of their Saviour. It was a conception long sanctified by time; the pagan mind needed no schooling to receive it; by embodying it in the 'mystery of the Mass', Christianity became the last and greatest of the mystery religions."[13]

A Christian Bishop has written, "Now we are so accustomed to these ideas that they seem to many Christians to belong to Christ's teaching. It comes as a shock to them to learn that at bottom such ideas are pagan, not Jewish."[14]

Zoroaster's Faith, well before the time of Christ, suffered the same infiltration of ideas from pagan beliefs. Reinach and Rawlinson both comment upon it. Zoroaster disapproved and detested the old Aryan custom of offering the juice of the intoxicating haoma plant to the gods, yet this ancient custom was gradually adopted into Zoroastrian belief after His death. The priests drank part of the liquid, and then shared the "remaining among the faithful in holy communion".

The Essenes, also before Christ, had a similar ritual meal. This sect of Judaism, according to Philo of Alexandria, Pliny the Elder, Josephus the Jewish historian, as well as the accounts of the Dead Sea Scrolls, not only had a sacred meal, but a rite of cleansing by water. The Essenes (Holy Ones) bathed in water as a "sacrament of purification". Then they partook of a sacred meal presided over by a priest who pronounced a "blessing with the first portion of the bread and wine".

Infant baptism was immediately followed by infant communion in the later days of the early Church, according to some sources. The two ceremonies were intimately and immediately connected. They were, in fact, considered as a single ceremony.

Cyprian refers to children who at the outset of their lives were taken to the Lord's table, and Augustine teaches that since *John* 6:53 shows that this sacrament (eucharist) is as essential to salvation as baptism, infants need this as much as the other. This practice continued for many centuries, and still exists in the Greek Orthodox Church. In the Roman Church it continued until the twelfth or thirteenth century.[15]

The Council of Trent (1560) decreed that children under the age of reason were not bound to observe this rite in this manner, and thus baptism and the eucharist were separated. However, baptism was still linked with the eucharist, but only by a *first communion*.

In the two rites of *baptism* and *confirmation* there can be seen a similarity to the two rites of *circumcision* and the *bar mitzvah* of the Jewish Faith.

Rowley states, "A Jewish boy enters potentially into the covenant at circumcision, but when he is 13 years of age, he has the bar mitzvah ceremony whereby he enters of his own volition into the life and faith of Israel, and is recognized as a loyal child of Judaism."[16]

In Christianity, the child, unable to participate intellectually in baptism, has this decision later ratified for him by the sacrament of confirmation.

When the convert in the early days of the Church was baptized and purified, he became a channel which was cleansed sufficiently to receive the Lord's Supper. His past sins were forgiven with baptism. The early Church had no instrument for forgiving later, or future sins, hence death-bed baptism became common. There was no sacrament of confession at that time. There was only public confession. At a later date, as mentioned earlier, one sin was permitted after baptism. Gradually more leniency became necessary. This eventually led to the Church doctrine of confession and absolution. It became a standardized procedure, and public confession gave way to private confession to the priest, who was authorized to dispense absolution for sins committed after the original baptism. "None the less," one Christian account relates, "for centuries the danger of sin after baptism was deemed so great that many Christians postponed baptism until they were at the point of death."[17]

The inability to perceive and accept the simple beauty of Christ's meaning of *the bread and the wine* led to centuries of such confusion with many quarrels and misunderstandings. It also led to new rites, which were introduced in order to resolve the problems which arose because of the development of the old rites.

As Durant says, in *The Age of Faith*, "The Church took literally the words ascribed to Christ at the Last Supper: of the bread, 'this is my body'; and of the wine: 'this is my blood'. The main feature of the Mass was the 'transubstantiation' of wafers of bread and a chalice of wine into the body and blood of Christ by the miraculous power of the priest; and the original purpose of the Mass was to allow the faithful to partake of the 'body and blood, soul and divinity', of the Second Person of the Triune God by eating the consecrated Host and drinking the consecrated wine. As the drinking of the transubstantiated wine risked spilling the blood of Christ, the custom arose in the twelfth century of communicating through taking only the Host; and when some conservatives (whose views were later adopted by the Hussites of Bohemia) demanded communion in both forms to make sure that they received the blood as well as the body of the Lord, theologians explained that the blood of Christ was 'concomitant' with His body in the bread, and His body was 'concomitant' with His blood in the wine. A thousand marvels were told of the power of the consecrated Host to cast out devils, cure diseases, stop fires, and detect perjury by choking liars. Every Christian was required to communicate at least once a year; and the First Communion of the young Christian was made an occasion of solemn pageantry and happy celebration."[18]

The catalogue of problems which arose from such a literal conception of the meaning of *baptism* and of *the bread and the wine* became greater with the passing of each century.

Leo IX presided over a Council at Reims which "forbade the clergy to receive fees for administering the eucharist, attending the sick or burying the dead".

Baptism by total immersion was changed for aspersion (sprinkling) before the tenth century as "less dangerous in northern climes".

The public confession of the early Church was replaced by private confession in the fourth century "to spare embarrassment to dignitaries".

By the eighth century the ecclesiastically authorized penances for each sin were established and published as a kind of spiritual system of double entry bookkeeping. These penances were lightened with time. Partial or plenary indulgences were granted by the Church. Confession absolved the sinner from the punishment of hell, but not from the temporal punishment in this world. This earthly punishment, however, *could* be removed by indulgences. Some cases of wholesale forgiveness of sin on this earthly plane were granted as early as the ninth century. Urban II offered the first plenary indulgence. It promised complete forgiveness of all sins to those who joined the First Crusade and fell in battle.

This plenary indulgence for all who should fall in war brought together an army of 30,000 men. The painful story of the Crusades and the wars with the Muslims need not be repeated here nor the shame that came as a result to the followers of two great religions, Christianity and Islám. Forgetful of the teachings on love and brotherhood commanded by each of their Founders, they participated enthusiastically in the mutual slaughter.

One brief account will suffice to demonstrate to what depths of degradation the lack of understanding concerning the inward truth of such doctrines can bring. It points out the sorrow that comes to those who blindly and slavishly follow the *outward*, material symbol rather than the *inward* spiritual truth. Baptism leads to the eucharist which leads to confession which leads to penance which leads to indulgence, and so on, *ad infinitum*. All are foreign to the simplicity, beauty and majesty of the teaching of His Holiness Christ. All are based on "vague and fragmentary" references which betray the very spirit of love and compassion in His words.

The Crusaders swarmed over the walls of Jerusalem on 15 July 1099, and according to Raymond of Agiles, a priest who was an eyewitness: ". . . wonderful things were to be seen. Numbers of the Saracens were beheaded . . . others were shot with arrows, or forced to jump from the towers; others were tortured for several days and then burned in flames. In the streets were seen piles of heads and hands and feet. One rode about everywhere amid the corpses of men and horses."[19]

Durant, in his *The Age of Faith*, adds: "Other contemporaries contribute details: women were stabbed to death, suckling babes were snatched by the leg from their mother's breasts and flung over the walls, or had their necks broken by being dashed against posts; and 70,000 Muslims remaining in the city were slaughtered. The surviving Jews were herded into a synagogue and burned alive. The victors flocked to the church of the Holy Sepulchre, whose grotto, they believed, had once held the crucified Christ. There, embracing one another, they wept with joy and release, and thanked the God of Mercies for their victory."[20]

Those who fell in the midst of such ecstatic slaughter received a plenary indulgence or complete forgiveness for all their past sins and rose in glory to the peace of heaven, according to the Church.

Thus "indulgences", which were at the outset designed to improve the earthly conduct of man, in reality led men astray – demoralizing both the giver and the receiver of the indulgence. The practice of granting indulgences grew alarmingly. Soon there arose the custom of "giving indulgences for repeating certain prayers, attending special religious services, building bridges, roads, churches or hospitals, clearing or draining swamps, contributing to a Crusade, to an ecclesiastical institution, a Church Jubilee or a Christian war. . . . The system was put to many good uses, but it opened the doors to human cupidity."[21]

A generation such as ours, which seldom questions the validity of its own traditional customs, is alarmed when it contemplates the history of events which gave them birth. It is even more alarming when we study the spreading net of complicated rituals and ceremonies which have arisen from the literal orthodox interpretation of those simple words of Christ: "he that cometh to me shall never hunger; and he that believeth on me shall never thirst."

History records that the Church "commissioned certain ecclesiastics, usually friars, as *quaestiarri* to raise funds by offering indulgences in return for gifts, repentance and prayer. These solicitors – whom the English called 'pardoners' – developed a competitive zeal that scandalized many Christians; they exhibited real or false relics to stimulate contributions; and they kept for themselves a due or undue part of their receipts. The Church made several efforts to reduce these abuses. The Fourth Lateran Council ordered bishops to warn the faithful against false relics and forged credentials; it ended the right of abbots, and limited that of bishops, to issue indulgences; and it called upon all ecclesiastics to exercise moderation in their zeal for the new device. In 1261 the Council of Mainz denounced many *quaestiarri* as wicked liars, who displayed the stray bones of men or beasts as those of saints, trained themselves to weep on order, and offered purgatorial bargains for a maximum of coin and a minimum of prayer. Similar condemnations were issued by church councils at Vienna (1311) and Ravenna (1317). The abuses continued."[22]

Confession, of course, was not a completely new concept arising with Christianity. In the practice of Mithraism at Eleusis, "the candidate was required to confess his sins". This public confession discouraged the Emperor Nero from participating. This public confession was adopted by Christianity and later altered to private confession to overcome the same problem which had faced Nero and other notables, namely embarrassment.

George Townshend, sometime Canon of St Patrick's Cathedral, Dublin, points out that Christ's appointment of the twelve Apostles to "bind" and "loose" was in no way associated with the right or privilege to forgive the individual sins of men, nor did this become a doctrine of the Church as private confession for nearly four centuries. It was, he said, an authority to carry on His teachings. To them He, Christ, "committed the evangelization of mankind ..." To them He gave "all the authority and discipline which would be needed for the prosecution of the task ... The spiritual future of mankind would depend on them and on those who after them would walk in their steps – the steps, that is, of humble faith ..."[23]

Yet these words, whose "sins ye shall forgive they are forgiven them," a mere fragment of the Gospels, have become the foundation for an elaborate doctrine which has caused a great cleavage in the ranks of Christ's holy Faith.

Bahá'u'lláh writes of confession:

> When the sinner findeth himself wholly detached and freed from all save God, he should beg forgiveness and pardon from Him. Confession of sins and transgressions before human beings is not permissible, as it hath never been nor will ever be conducive to divine forgiveness. Moreover such confession before people results in one's humiliation and abasement, and God – exalted be His glory – wisheth not the humiliation of His servants. Verily He is the Compassionate, the Merciful.[24]

It is not the purpose here to find fault with the sincere efforts of any religion to protect and to help its followers. Without doubt there have been many devoted and sacrificial attempts made to purify the inward life of Christianity. The grave obstacle which eventually proved to be insurmountable was the simple truth that the pure waters of the Fountain of Christ had gradually become tainted with compromise at their source. Whatever flowed out, in whatever direction, became increasingly discoloured and clouded by such compromise.

The Church fathers themselves were appalled at the divisions which decimated even the very early Church; and all because of these differences in a literal interpretation of doctrine. Irenaeus counted twenty varieties of Christianity in the year A.D. 187 (approximate), and by A.D. 384 Epiphanius listed eighty.[25]

Bahá'u'lláh's teachings repeatedly explain that it is the *inner meaning* which is important, and not the outward event. This is the lesson which man has failed to learn and with tragic consequences. The teachings of Christ were capable of purifying the spirit of man. They provided the real food and nourishment for those who believed. Considered from this viewpoint, the story of the *Last Supper* becomes an eternal analogy which can teach man down through the ages.

> And as they were eating, Jesus took bread, and blessed it, and brake it, and gave it to the disciples, and said, Take, eat; this is my body.
> And he took the cup, and gave thanks, and gave it to them, saying, Drink ye all of it;
> For this is my blood ... [26]

Reflect. How clear is Christ's symbology: as man is physically fed by food and drink, so is his spirit nourished by spiritual food and drink – the "bread of heavenly teachings" taken with the "wine of belief". Christ was not physically transformed into bread and wine before their eyes. If He had been, He could not have remained with them in person. The Writings of the Bahá'í Faith state:

> The disciples had taken many meals from the hand of Christ; why was the last supper distinguished from the others? It is evident that the heavenly bread did not signify this material bread, but rather the divine nourishment of the spiritual body of Christ, the divine graces and heavenly perfections of which his disciples partook, and with which they became filled. [27]

Jesus knew that His hour of departure was at hand. He wished to leave an unforgettable symbol by which His disciples would always remember the importance of the Spirit of His teachings.

His lesson said: "Approach the Word of God (Christ) and believe." He told them: "This is my body and blood by which all men must be fed. He who eats of this food (these teachings) will never die because it nourishes the spirit which is everlasting; whosoever does not eat of it, is already dead; although physically he may have the appearance of life."

Jesus told His disciples that if they ate His flesh and blood they would have eternal life. There could be no doubt that He was speaking of the "heavenly food" of His teachings which came from God, for He said:

Labour not for the meat which perisheth, but for that *meat* which endureth unto everlasting life, which the Son of man shall give unto you ... [28]

In the very next verse they asked Him:

What shall we do, that we might work the works of God?

Christ had already told them:

My *meat* is to do the will of Him that sent me and to finish his work.

Now to their question, Christ answered:

This is the work of God, that ye *believe* on him whom he hath sent. [29]

This was the "bread" and "wine" they should eat and drink: *Belief* in the Messenger of God. The physical bread or physical flesh was nothing more than a figurative way of conveying this inner truth. The New Testament clearly states:

... flesh and blood cannot inherit the kingdom of God; [30]

No one made this fact plainer than Christ Himself. In one single chapter He says over and over:

I am that *bread* of life ... This is the *bread* which cometh down

from heaven, that a man may eat thereof, and not die ...
For my flesh is *meat* indeed, and my blood is *drink* indeed.[31]

This is stated by Christ in the same chapter in which He warned the people not to labour for "the meat which perisheth". Still, they did not understand Him. Even His own disciples whom He had taught so patiently could not comprehend this inward truth.

Many therefore of his disciples, when they had heard this, said, This is an hard saying; who can hear it?

Christ said:

Doth this offend you?

Then Jesus tried yet another way of helping them to understand:

It is the spirit that quickeneth; the flesh profiteth nothing: the words that I speak unto you, *they* are spirit, and *they* are life.[32]

Yet, in spite of His repeated lesson, His tenderness, His patience, and His love, it is written of His followers:

From that time many of his disciples went back, and walked no more with him.[33]

Failure to understand these outward symbols or their relation to an inward truth led many in that day to deny Christ and to refuse His Message. We can well imagine the confusion and misunderstanding that would exist 2,000 years later!

Differences of opinion regarding the meaning of the *Last Supper*, and as to whether it should be interpreted physically or figuratively, resulted in disputes which have indeed lasted for centuries. These quarrels have divided His Church, and varied its form and belief until they would be beyond the recognition of His Holiness Christ Himself.

History has shown that "the question whether the Eucharist was Jesus' flesh and blood *in fact*, or only *after a manner*, remained to be bitterly debated long after the Reformation".[34]

The longer the time that passed, the less comprehension there seemed to be concerning the beautiful truth behind this outer symbol of the bread and the wine.

This day in which we are now living is the long-promised day of "the one fold and the one shepherd". Bahá'u'lláh has come to *unseal* the meaning of the sacred Scriptures. His purpose is to renew and restate the inward truth of these doctrines. Only in this way can all the separated and divided segments of religions and nations once more be bound together in unity. Bahá'u'lláh's teachings deal with the spiritual and material needs of both the individual human being and the nation to which he belongs. For this reason, the Bahá'í teachings speak in detail of the true meaning of these various doctrines of His Holiness Christ.

Bahá'u'lláh urges us, throughout His Writings, to "look into all things with a searching eye". Let no man be deceived by the outer shell, while ignoring the inner, living body of truth, He tells us.

Man falls into his gravest errors, the Bahá'í Writings explain, when he permits the *outward symbol* to become more important than the *inward truth* for which it stands.

This explanation has been but a glimmering of the reality of Christ's teachings, and of the pearls that lie hidden in the ocean of Bahá'u'lláh's utterance. Bahá'u'lláh has written:*

Know assuredly that just as thou firmly believest that the Word of God, exalted be His glory, endureth for ever, thou must, likewise, believe with undoubting faith that its meaning can never be exhausted. They who are its appointed interpreters [Messengers], they whose hearts are the repositories of its secrets, are, however, the only ones who can comprehend its

---

* See *Kitáb-i-Íqan* (Book of Certitude), *Hidden Words, Seven Valleys, Gleanings From the Writings of Bahá'u'lláh*, and *Prayers and Meditations*, which are among the more important books of the over one hundred volumes Bahá'u'lláh has written for the guidance of modern-day society.

manifold wisdom. Whoso, while reading the Sacred Scriptures, is tempted to choose therefrom whatever may suit him with which to challenge the authority of the Representative of God among men, is, indeed, as one dead, though to outward seeming he may walk and converse with his neighbours, and share with them their food and their drink.[35]

For this same reason Christ said that those who did not believe in Him were "dead". Bahá'u'lláh adds:

Oh, would that the world could believe Me! Were all the things that lie enshrined within the heart of Bahá [Bahá'u'lláh], and which the Lord, His God, the Lord of all names, hath taught Him, to be unveiled to mankind, every man on earth would be dumbfounded.

How great the multitude of truths which the garment of words can never contain! How vast the number of such verities as no expression can adequately describe ... [36]

In conveying spiritual truths, Bahá'u'lláh's teachings tell us, our speech is as ineffective as the cry of animals trying to communicate with the human kingdom. We shall understand this more clearly as we explore next the meaning of the symbol: Jesus, the Son of God.

CHAPTER SIX

THE MEANING OF: JESUS, SON OF GOD

Misunderstanding about the reality of the station of Christ has caused great difficulties among Christians for over nineteen centuries. It has even caused grave separation among His followers. Christ's station has been described as everything from that of a human reformer and teacher to that of the physical Son of God, even as that of God Himself.

The very symbol used by the early Christians called attention to Christ's exalted station. When the sign of the *fish* was secretly used to identify Christian believers to each other (approximately A.D. 180), it was chosen, we are told, "because the Greek word for it [fish], I-CH-TH-U-S, formed the initials of the phrase *Iesous Christus theou uios soter* – 'Jesus Christ, Son of God, Saviour.'"[1]

Christians now find it exceedingly difficult to believe in or to accept any new Messenger of God, because of their misunderstanding of the station of Christ. Although Jesus Himself clearly promised that One *would* come after him, and referred to His own return in over 250 separate New Testament passages,* Christians still insist:

"Other Messengers or Prophets are of much less importance than Christ. They are mere teachers, but Jesus is the Son of God. No other station can rank as high as that."

This attitude is reminiscent of what the people said at the time of Christ. They took this very same position in relation to Moses. When they were told about a new Messenger of God called Jesus of Nazareth, they answered:

---

* See *Thief in the Night*, pp. 66–71.

"He is but a poor, unlearned teacher. Moses was the *Interlocutor*, the Mouthpiece of God. He actually talked with God and heard His voice in the Holy Mountain. No other station can rank as high as this."

Once again we find the *outward symbol* blinding the people to the *inward truth*.

Christ wished to show the close relationship which existed between the Messenger or Prophet and God. Therefore, He used the clear symbol of the son; the only son, who is granted special privileges in speaking for the father. In this light His explanations were readily understandable.

The Apostles and later followers believed that the parable of the vineyard demonstrated the validity of the Mission of Christ, the Son, in representing God. Christ's *symbolical* explanation of the relationship between Messenger and God was taken *literally*. This led to the belief among some that Christ was the actual, physical son of God, His only son. "Jesus", they said, "must be believed in, and accepted, not because of the great teachings which He brought, but because He was the only begotten Son of God." They ignored the fact that this concept was in direct contradiction to Christ's own words.

Jesus became supreme for these followers, not for the reason He Himself gave, namely His teachings and the spirit of love and brotherhood which He brought as a Messenger of God, but because His followers believed that He, Christ, was the actual Son of God.

Bahá'u'lláh assures us that it was the Holy Spirit reflected in Christ which was the means of His honour and greatness. It was not the person of Jesus that was important, but the Holy Spirit of Christ which shone within Him. The same principle was true of Moses. It is true of every Messenger of God. They are all Mirrors that reflect the light of the Sun of God's truth. If the light does not shine within Them, they are merely frames and glass, nothing more.

The Writings of the Bahá'í Faith state:

That which causes honour and greatness, is the splendour and bounty of the divine perfections ... The splendour and honour of the holy souls and the Divine Manifestations [Messengers] come from their heavenly perfections, bounties, and glory, and from nothing else.[2]

This is true of all the Founders of the great religions: Krishna, Moses, Zoroaster, Buddha, Christ, Muhammad, the Báb, and Bahá'u'lláh. However, for the sake of simplicity, and because this book is directed to the Christian world, we shall speak in these pages mostly of Moses, Christ, and Bahá'u'lláh.

Bahá'u'lláh points out that with the coming of each Messenger of God, His followers mistake the outward form for the inward reality. Hence they elevate His person to a station which was never intended by the Founder Himself.

Christ expressed this theme of the sun (God) and the mirror (Messenger) with great clarity to His own disciples. He said:

If ye had known me, ye should have known my Father also . . . he that hath seen me hath seen the Father . . . [3]

Unfortunately, these and other similar words were taken literally, and gradually the Church doctrine of the *Son of God* was built upon them.

Yet Jesus Himself, in the verse which follows the one just quoted, makes it quite clear that it is the light in the mirror, the Spirit within, that is the all-important thing. He told them:

. . . I speak not of myself: but the Father that dwelleth in me, he doeth the works.[4]

It is the sun shining within the mirror that is responsible for the light. It is not the mirror itself. Had the followers of Christ understood this inner truth, they would have "watched" for His return *in the last days* as He had commanded them. In this same chapter, Christ speaks several times of His own return, and twice mentions the *Comforter* whom God would send. Christ also mentions the "unsealing" of His own words by this Comforter:

... he shall teach you all things, and bring all things to your remembrance, whatsoever I have said unto you.[5]

The sun that shines in the mirror on Saturday is the same sun that shines in the mirror on Sunday and Monday. Thus the light of God that was reflected in each of the Prophets was one and the same. From the day of Abraham to that of Christ, the same sunlight of God shone in each of His Mirrors or Messengers. Unable to understand this, the people stoned Christ:

Then said the Jews unto him, Thou art not yet fifty years old, and hast thou seen Abraham?

Jesus said unto them, Verily, verily, I say unto you, Before Abraham was, I am.

Then took they up stones to cast at him: but Jesus hid himself, and went out of the temple ... [6]

Christ was speaking of the light of the sun (God), not the light in the mirror (Messenger). The light of God's Sun of Truth shining in the mirror of Christ did indeed exist and shine from the beginning of time in the Mirror of other Messengers. Hence, Jesus might well say, with unquestionable truth when speaking of that light: "Before Abraham was, I am."

An almost identical story is told of Krishna, long before the days of Jesus, the Christ. In the *Song of God*, the *Bhagavad-Gita*, Krishna speaks to his disciple, Arjuna:

I taught this yoga first to Vivaswat ...

Arjuna replies:

Vivaswat was born long before you. How am I to believe that you were the first to teach this yoga?

Krishna explains:

I am the birthless, the deathless ...
In every age I come back
To deliver the holy,
To destroy the sin of the sinner,
To establish righteousness.

Swami Prabhavananda and Christopher Isherwood, in their translation of the *Bhagavad-Gita*, say: "Hinduism accepts the belief in
many divine incarnations, including Krishna, Buddha and Jesus
and foresees that there will be many more."[7]

Krishna spoke of the difficulty of making the people of His day
understand the inward truth behind the outward symbols. He said:

Those who lack discrimination may quote the letter of the
scriptures, but they are really denying its inner truth. They are
full of worldly desires, and hungry for the rewards of heaven
... they teach elaborate rituals which are supposed to obtain
pleasures and power for those who perform them.

Krishna spoke almost the same words as Christ in trying to get
His followers to seek the inward truth. He said:

I am ... the Word that is God ... I am the path ...

Yet the people could not see that He was speaking of the light
within, and not of His physical person. This was the *inward* meaning of the *outward* symbol of these words spoken by both Krishna
and Christ.

Surely the people should have understood that Christ was deliv-
ering the Message given to Him by God when He said, "Before
Abraham was, I am." This same "I am", or Holy Spirit, was the one
that spoke to Moses saying:

I AM THAT I AM . . .Thus shalt thou say unto the children
of Israel, *I Am* hath sent me unto you ... This is my name
forever, unto all generations.[8]

This was confirmed again when the Voice (Ahura Mazda) spoke to Zoroaster:

> My name is *I Am* . . . I am the Keeper, the Creator, and Maintainer; I am the Discerner, I am the Most Beneficent Spirit.

The teachings of the Bahá'í Faith tell us that Christ was speaking of the Holy Spirit within Him, the "I Am", the light of the sun shining in the mirror; the eternal sun which had existed from the beginning. Christ was not referring to His physical body. This is why He said: "Before Abraham was, I am."

The difference between His inner Spirit and His outer self, Christ made clear in the words:

> . . . Why callest thou me good? there is none good but one, that is, God . . . [9]

Bahá'u'lláh also spoke of this spiritual sunlight which is reflected in God's perfect Mirrors, the Messengers of God. He testifies to its power, saying:

> Know verily that whenever this Youth turneth His eyes toward His own self, He findeth it the most insignificant of all creation. When he contemplates, however, the bright effulgences He hath been empowered to manifest, lo, that self is transfigured before Him into a sovereign Potency permeating the essence of all things visible and invisible.[10]

Thus in every age, Bahá'u'lláh tells us, each Messenger Who appears is both the "first" and the "last". He is the Alpha and the Omega, for He is referring to the Holy Spirit which dwells within – the sunlight in the mirror – and it is the same in every age.

Bahá'u'lláh, in his *Book of Certitude*, repeatedly refers to such symbols, pointing out that man has ignored the greatness of the *Spirit* while exalting that of the *Flesh*:

If one will ponder but for a while ... one will surely discover all mysteries hidden in the terms "grave", "tomb", ... "paradise", and "hell". But oh! how strange and pitiful! Behold, all the people are imprisoned within the tomb of self, and lie buried beneath the nethermost depths of worldly desire! Wert thou to attain to but a dewdrop of the crystal waters of divine knowledge, thou wouldst readily realize that true life is not the life of the flesh but the life of the spirit. For the life of the flesh is common to both men and animals, whereas the life of the spirit is possessed only by the pure in heart who have quaffed from the ocean of faith and partaken of the fruit of certitude. This life knoweth no death, and this existence is crowned by immortality ... If by "life" be meant this earthly life, it is evident that death must needs overtake it.[11]

We have dealt generally with the title *Son of God*. We have shown that it is a title which is symbolic of one who represents the Father. Let us now be more specific. Let us examine the Old and the New Testament in an effort to determine the true meaning of the term itself: "Son of God".

Although Christ made His own relationship to Almighty God crystal clear, still it has been misunderstood, misrepresented, and misinterpreted for centuries. Those to whom Christ first spoke of this relationship thought He referred to Himself as a person and not to the Spirit within Him. These people objected violently. They became outraged and stoned Christ. They said He claimed to be God.

Christ said:

I and my Father are one.[12]

The Sun and the Mirror are one with regard to the light: this was His meaning. Yet he was misunderstood, for the Gospel records:

Then the Jews took up stones again to stone him.

    Jesus answered them ... for which of those [good works] do ye stone me?

The Jews answered him, saying, For a good work we stone thee not; but for *blasphemy*; and because that thou, being a man, makest thyself God.[13]

Then Christ exposed their lack of understanding of His words. He said:

Is it not written in your law, I said, *Ye are gods*?

If he called them *gods*, unto whom the word of God came, and the scripture cannot be broken:

Say ye of him, whom the Father hath sanctified, and sent into the world, Thou blasphemest; because I said, I am the *Son of God*? ...

Therefore they sought again to take him: but he escaped out of their hand ... [14]

He, Christ, was the mirror; God was the sun that shone in that mirror. They were thus one as to the light, but not as to essence. The mirror was not, and never could be, the sun itself. This was the lesson Christ taught.

Jesus tried in every way to make sure that this truth would not be misunderstood. The people sought "to kill him, because he not only had broken the sabbath, but said also that God was his Father, making himself equal with God". Christ tried to show them their error and that He was but an instrument of God: that He did not in any way consider Himself the equal of God; nor had He any power that was not God-given. He insisted:

Verily, verily, I say unto you, The Son can do nothing of himself, but what he seeth the Father do: for what things soever he doeth, these also doeth the Son likewise.[15]

He again assured the people:

For I have not spoken of myself; but the Father which sent me, he gave me a commandment, what I should say, and what I should speak.[16]

It was not sufficient for them. Christ was a blasphemer and in no way what they expected. Bahá'u'lláh has written that the people in every age deny the Messenger of God because He does not appear in the manner they expect. He says:

> Were these [people] to ask the Light of Truth [Messengers] concerning those images which their idle fancy hath carved, and were they to find His answer inconsistent with their own conceptions and their own understanding of the Book, they would assuredly denounce Him Who is the Mine and Wellhead of all Knowledge as the very negation of understanding. Such things have happened in every age.[17]

When they "denounced" Christ for *blasphemy* and for *breaking the Sabbath*, Jesus pointed out that they did not understand their own Scripture. Christ accused them of interpreting it as they wished, and from an *outward*, not an *inward*, point of view. He told them:

> Search the scriptures; for in them ye think ye have eternal life: and they are they which testify of me.
>   And ye will not come to me, that ye might have life...
>   I am come in my Father's name, and ye receive me not
> ...[18]

Bahá'u'lláh spoke of those same misguided ones who, in every age, insist that God's Messenger conform to their own limited standard. Bahá'u'lláh pointed out that despite the fact that He had "unsealed" the Books so that all might understand the Truth, the people in this day were still acting as they had acted in the day of Christ. He warned:

> ... it behooveth no man to interpret the holy words according to his own imperfect understanding, nor, having found

them to be contrary to his inclination and desires, to reject and repudiate their truth. For such, today, is the manner of the divines [religious leaders] and doctors of the age, who occupy the seats of knowledge and learning, and who have named ignorance knowledge, and called oppression justice.[19]

Christ's words show clearly that they had done the same thing to Him:

Do not think that I will accuse you to the Father: there is one that accuseth you, even Moses, in whom ye trust.

For had ye believed Moses, ye would have believed me: for he wrote of me.

But if ye believe not his writings, how shall ye believe my words?[20]

Bahá'u'lláh has called attention to the tragedy which, unhappily, takes place with the appearance of each new Prophet. The people remember the former Mirror, but forget the Light that shone in that Mirror. They are misled because the name, and the outer physical characteristics, of the new Messenger are different. They fail utterly to see that the inner Spirit is exactly the same. They remember the Messenger, but they have forgotten the Message which He brought.

Thus the Christians, like the people before them, exalted Christ, the Messenger of their Faith, while neglecting His Message. They began to worship the Mirror of Jesus instead of the Light of Christ within. The station with which they invested Christ as the actual Son of God, because of their love for Him, now became an obstacle to their own spiritual progress.

Consider: If Christ's greatness were to lie in the fact that He was born of a mother only, having no father, then Adam must be considered greater than Christ; for Adam had neither father nor mother. Whether Adam came into existence slowly or immediately, he was without parents.

This same station of superior greatness must also be awarded to Melchizedek, for he also was without parents, and he was also called the Son of God, and a king of righteousness and a king of peace:

> Without father, without mother, without descent, having nei-
> ther beginning of days, nor end of life; but made like unto *the
> Son of God:*[21]

We can find other examples where this station, the Son of God, was
attributed symbolically to others beside Christ. When we trace the
lineage of Jesus, we find this same station bestowed upon Adam:

> Which was the son of Enos, which was the son of Seth, which
> was the son of Adam, which was *the son of God.*[22]

The privilege of becoming sons of God was given even to the followers of Christ, under certain conditions:

> But as many as received him, to them gave he power to become
> *the sons of God*, even to them that believe on his name.[23]

In the Old Testament, it is pointed out that the sincere and faithful
believers are gods and the sons of God:

> God standeth in the congregation of the mighty; he judgeth
> among the gods.[24]

Or in yet another way, the verse which Christ himself quoted:

> I have said, Ye are gods; and all of *you are children of the most
> High.*[25]

In the New Testament it is written of the faithful believers:

> Behold, what manner of love the Father hath bestowed upon
> us, that we should be called *the sons of God:*[26]

And in the closing Book of the Bible, *Revelation*, it is established once and for all that this term "Son of God" is a symbolic term. It is a station which is reached by belief in God and in drawing close to His teachings and His Works:

He that overcometh shall inherit all things; and I will be his God, and *he shall be my son.*[27]

The teachings of the Bahá'í Faith make it quite clear that there is a vast difference between the station of the followers of Christ, and that of Christ Himself. It is not the intention of the examples given above to imply that these followers are in any respect His equal. The respect, love and reverence which the members of the Bahá'í Faith have for Christ is unequalled, and in most cases even unapproached, in the Christian congregations of the present day.

God is the *Sun, Christ and the other Messengers of God* are the *Rays* of the *Sun*, and their followers are the *earth*. The *Sun* through its *Rays* brings life and light to the *earth*. The Messengers of God are in this way the source of all of man's spiritual life. Hence, Christ said, "I am the Way, the Truth and the Light, and no one cometh unto the Father except through Me." Christ was the rays of the sun in that day. There was no other source of life or light except in the warmth, heat, and brightness of His, Christ's, teachings.

The intent of such examples is to show that these terms are *outward symbols* of *inward truths*. These examples prove that becoming a Son of God is a spiritual, not a physical thing. These verses make it obvious that the true being of a disciple is created by a spiritual reality, and not by a physical power.

Verse twelve of the first chapter of *John* confers the station:

As many as received him, to them gave he power to become *the sons of God* ....

Verse thirteen shows that this station is solely a spiritual one:

... Which were born, not of blood, *nor of the will of the flesh,* nor of the will of man, *but of God.*

The disciples were born of human parents, but their true *being* (that of the spirit) was born of their belief in God through the acceptance of Christ and His Message. This is one *inward* meaning of the phrase "son of God".

As it applied to Jesus, it had even a richer significance. As all men are children of one God, and members of one human family, the eldest son commands special honour and respect. This place of honour was the station of Christ. This is another *inward* truth. There are even greater meanings. The Writings of the Faith of Bahá'u'lláh state:

> But as Christ found existence through the Spirit of God, He called Himself the Son of God.[28]

This is a glimpse of the *inner* truth behind the *outer* symbol "Son of God". These are just a few leaves taken from the tree of Bahá'u'lláh's explanations. Bahá'u'lláh Himself says of the great variety of examples which He gives in His *Book of Certitude*:

> All these things which We have repeatedly mentioned, and the details which we have cited from divers sources, have no other purpose but to enable thee to grasp the meaning of the allusions in the utterances of the chosen Ones of God, lest certain of these utterances cause thy feet to falter and thy heart to be dismayed.[29]

Christ came in the station of the Son, and was misunderstood. Bahá'u'lláh has come in the station of the Father and was misunderstood. Both stations are symbols. The Jews refused to accept Jesus when He came in the station of the *Son* because they clung to the old outward form. The Christians in this day refuse to accept Bahá'u'lláh, Who has come in the station of the *Father*, for the same reason.

We shall now examine the *inner* meaning of the symbolical station of the *Father*.

CHAPTER SEVEN

IN THE GLORY OF THE FATHER

The stations of both the *Father* and the *Son* are, as mentioned in the Scriptures, figurative. Jesus is not God because He is called the *Son*. Bahá'u'lláh is not God because He is called the *Father*. To express such a thought would be blasphemy, and contrary to all the teachings of the Bahá'í Faith.

These titles are nothing more than explanations of the relationship of Christ and Bahá'u'lláh to the infinite, unknowable, Almighty God, the Supreme Being who uncovers for men the brightness of His glory and knowledge through His Messengers and Prophets in successive ages.

Jesus represented God as the Son, the heir of the Kingdom. Bahá'u'lláh came as the Father. In this day of the "one fold and one shepherd", Bahá'u'lláh is the *Father* who gathers together all the religions, nations, and races: just as a father gathers all his children. He is the promised Shepherd of the "one fold", prophesied for the last days in the sacred Scriptures.

Christ clearly foretold that in the coming day of the *Father*, Who would be the shepherd of all the sheep, there would be other lambs (believers) in addition to the Christians. Jesus said:

> And other sheep I have, which are not of this fold: them also I must bring, and they shall hear my voice; and there shall be one fold, and one shepherd.[1]

Ezekiel speaks of this same day, appointing it *at the time of the end*. It will take place, he says, when the children of Israel will be gathered from all nations as lambs by the One Great Shepherd. The Jews were scattered throughout the world in A.D. 70 when Titus destroyed Jerusalem. Since this event took place *after* Christ's crucifixion, it was clear that Ezekiel's promise was for the *latter days* of the *Father*; a day of which Ezekiel spoke when he said:

> And I will bring them out from the people, and gather them from the countries, and will bring them to their own land, and feed them upon the mountains of Israel...[2]

This flock of Israel began to gather after twelve centuries of separation. The Jews were finally permitted to return to Israel in 1844 with the signing of the Edict of Toleration. The faith of Bahá'u'lláh, the Shepherd and Father of the flock, began in that same exact year, 1844.* Ezekiel promised:

> And I will set up one shepherd over them, and he shall feed them, even my servant David; he shall feed them, and he shall be their shepherd ... And I will make with them a covenant of peace ...[3]

This servant David (Beloved) of the time of the end was Bahá'u'lláh. Bahá'u'lláh wrote to the kings and rulers of the world on behalf of the "sheep" of the "other folds". He called upon those rulers of the world to unite and establish a "covenant of peace" so that the flock of God might be protected.

Isaiah spoke of this same *Father* of the children of Israel, this good shepherd:

> Behold, the Lord God will come with strong hand ... He shall feed his flock like a shepherd: he shall gather the lambs with his arm ...[4]

---

* For this unique and surprising story of how the Jews were permitted to return to their homeland by *The Edict of Toleration*, signed in almost the exact hour of the birth of the Bahá'í Faith, fulfilling the prophecy of Christ, that He would return to earth when "the times of the Gentiles" were fulfilled, read *Thief in the Night*, pp. 11–16.

In that *same* chapter, just *five* verses earlier, Isaiah promises that in that day:

> . . . *the glory of the Lord* shall be revealed, and all flesh shall see it together: for the mouth of the Lord hath spoken it.[5]

Bahá'u'lláh, Whose name means *the Glory of the Lord*, or *the Glory of God*, called Himself the Father, just as Christ had called Himself the Son. Both titles are symbolical. Bahá'u'lláh's Mission was to gather all of the peoples of the world into one moral, peace-loving, prosperous world society. To establish the "oneness of God, the oneness of His Messengers, and the oneness of His children" was the purpose of Bahá'u'lláh's life. The very administrative headquarters in which the work of His Faith is carried out in thousands of centres in all parts of the world is called "the sacred fold". In these "sacred folds" the sheep receive the food of His teachings.

Micah prophesied:

> In that day also he shall come even to thee from Assyria . . . [6]

Bahá'u'lláh came from Persia (once part of the ancient kingdom of Assyria).

Micah further prophesied that God would command this Messiah to:

> Feed thy people with thy rod, the flock of thine heritage, which dwell solitarily in the wood, *in the midst of Carmel*:[7]

The World Centre of Bahá'u'lláh's Faith is in the midst of Carmel. From this centre, the *rod* of His teachings goes out into every "sacred fold" in all parts of the planet.

Micah concludes by saying of this Messiah of the *last days*, that for forty years, a period equal to the number of years that the Jews were "coming out of the land of Egypt", God would:

> shew unto him marvellous things.[8]

Bahá'u'lláh's Mission began in 1852. It ended in 1892 – exactly "forty years", as foretold.

Furthermore, speaking of this same Mount Carmel, Isaiah declared:

> . . . Carmel and Sharon, they shall see *the glory of the Lord*, and the excellency of our God.[9]

Isaiah foretells that this will take place on the day when the "ransomed of the Lord" return to Israel. For the purpose of this book, concerning the meanings hidden in the Scriptures, Isaiah makes a statement of even more significance, for in this same chapter, he says that when *the glory of the Lord* appears:

> Then the eyes of the blind shall be opened, and the ears of the deaf shall be unstopped.[10]

Bahá'u'lláh, whose name means *the Glory of the Lord*, leaves no doubt as to who is meant by these words of Isaiah. With His own pen Bahá'u'lláh records:

> I am the One Whom the tongue of Isaiah hath extolled, the One with Whose name both the Torah and the Evangel [Gospels] were adorned.[11]

Bahá'u'lláh, the Father, has unsealed the Books and clearly explained these long misunderstood truths. A careful examination of His teachings by a sincere seeker will reveal a "fountain of the refreshing water of truth", which will indeed open the eyes of the blind and unstop the ears of the deaf.

The symbolical meaning of the *Son* and the *Father* is set down in unmistakable terms in Christ's own *Parable of the Vineyard*.

> A certain man planted a vineyard, and set an hedge about it, and digged a place for the winefat, and built a tower, and let it out to husbandmen, and went into a far country.

And at the season he sent to the husbandmen a servant, that he might receive from the husbandmen of the fruit of the vineyard.

And they caught *him*, and beat him, and sent him away empty.

And again he sent unto them *another* servant; and at him they cast stones, and wounded him in the head, and sent him away shamefully handled.

And again he sent *another*; and him they killed, and *many others*; beating some, and killing some.

Having yet therefore one son, his wellbeloved, he sent him also last unto them, saying, They will reverence my son.

But those husbandmen said among themselves, This is the heir; come, let us kill him, and the inheritance shall be ours.

And they took *him*, and killed him, and cast him out of the vineyard.

What shall therefore the *lord of the* vineyard do? he will come and destroy the husbandmen, and will give the vineyard unto others.[12]

The meaning is this:

The *vineyard* is the earth. The man who planted it is God. The *husbandmen* to whom it was let out are the people of the earth, especially the religious leaders.

The *servant* who was sent into the vineyard (earth) was the Messenger or Prophet of God. He came to receive from the people of the earth the fruit of the vineyard: i.e. the hearts of the people, hearts which believed in God and in His Messenger and both loved and served their fellowmen.

The *husbandmen* (people and religious leaders) denied the Messenger. They beat him and drove him off. So God sent another servant (prophet) into the vineyard (earth) to claim His right from His creation. But the husbandmen (people and leaders) stoned him; they beat and killed the others as they came.

Finally, the owner of the vineyard (God) sent His son (Christ) into the vineyard (earth). He thought: Surely they will honour

Him, My Son, and at last know the truth. They crucified Him.

Then, according to the parable, the Lord of the Vineyard (Bahá'u'lláh) came into the vineyard himself to destroy the husbandmen. Bahá'u'lláh came in the station of *the Father* as Christ came in that of *the Son*. Their Mission was one: to bring the Word of God to humanity.

The entire history of religion is told in this one, brief parable.

The servants or *Messengers* of God are many, but their Mission is one. The speakers, Messengers of God, are many, but the Word is one. The chapters vary, but they are all parts of the same unfolding progressive Book of God. There are many lamps (Messengers) but the same light shines in each of them.

In this day, the planet has been shrivelled to the size of a pea. We can speak around the world in a flash. We can see around the world in an instant. We can travel around the world in hours. The earth has become one small neighbourhood, one family. Hence the need for one Father. Bahá'u'lláh, the *Lord of the Vineyard*, has come that all the children of God may know and understand the Message of God for today. Bahá'u'lláh is the Shepherd of *all* the sheep from whatever flock they may have come.

Just as the station *Son of God* has blinded the Christians to the Light of Bahá'u'lláh's truth, in like manner the station *Seal of the Prophets*, attributed to Muhammad by the Muslims, has kept the people of Islám from recognizing and accepting the Father and Shepherd of the flock, Bahá'u'lláh.

Yet a study of their sacred Book, the Qur'án, reveals that Muhammad never once implied that He (meaning the Holy Spirit within) would *not* return.

There are two main classes of Prophets referred to in the Qur'án. One is called *Nábí* and the other is called *Rasúl*. *Nábí* are the prophets who foretell events to come and make prophecies of the future. *Rasúl* is the Messenger Who brings a Book and teachings.

Muhammad, when He referred to Himself as the *Seal* of the Prophets, referred always to *Nábí*, never to *Rasúl*. His own words show that the *Rasúl* (Messengers) of God will come continuously. He was the *Seal* of the *Nábí*, for the time of such prophecy was past. With the coming of the "one fold, and one shepherd" and the uniting of all mankind into one flock of God, there was no longer the need for Prophets to speak and prophesy of that great day yet to come. It had arrived. Bahá'u'lláh Himself declared:

> He Who is the Seal of the Prophets hath said: "Increase my wonder and amazement at Thee, O God!" ... I testify that, through Thy Revelation, the things hidden in the Books of God have been revealed, and that whatsoever hath been recorded by Thy Messengers in the sacred Scriptures hath been fulfilled.[13]

Not only Christianity and Judaism spoke of the coming of that great day when there would be one Father for all the people, and one Shepherd for all the flocks. Hinduism, Zoroastrianism, Buddhism, and Islám all refer to this convergence of faith in one Fold in the last days.

Zoroastrianism is particularly rich in this theme of the promised Father or Redeemer Who would come from Persia (the homeland of Bahá'u'lláh).

This entire story of the coming of the Father, with its references from *Daniel, Ezekiel, Jeremiah, Micah, Isaiah, Hosea*, the *Sibylline Books* and classical literature, is told in its full richness in *Thief in the Night* (pp. 107–77).

The following are a few fresh and intriguing words from the prophecies of Zoroaster's Faith concerning the great Shepherd and Father of mankind. It is written of His coming:

1. God will give you [Persia] a good ending.
2. I will send someone from this nation [Persia] Who will renew religion.
3. When Persia and the other countries are overtaken by the Arabs, I will choose one from the generation of the Kings of Persia, so that He will call the people of the world from East to West to worship one God.[14]

Bahá'u'lláh was descended from the line of kings of the Sassanian dynasty of Persia. He was also descended from the line of Zoroaster Himself. M. N. Dhalla, High Priest of the Parsees of northwestern India, in his *Zoroastrian Theology*, speaks of Zoroaster's "own kith and kin, a superman of miraculous powers" who would come "to renovate the world".[15]

"Zoroaster", Dhalla says, "postulated a renovation of the universe, a new dispensation in which the world will become perfect at the last days."[16]

Plutarch also spoke of the ancient Persians' "belief that at the time of the Renovation, mankind will speak one language and have one commonwealth".[17]

Miles Dawson, in his *The Ethical Religion of Zoroaster*, points out that according to Zoroastrian scriptures, ". . . the birth of Zarathustra (Zoroaster) began the last world-epoch of three thousand years; after three prophets of his seed have, at intervals, carried his doctrine throughout the world, the *Last Judgment* will be pronounced, the Kingdom of Ahura-Mazda will come . . ."[18]

It is now approximately, perhaps exactly, three thousand years since the appearance of Zoroaster. Three great Messengers of God, Buddha, Christ and Muhammad, of the same "spiritual seed" as Zoroaster, have carried the Word of God into the "easts of the earth and the wests thereof." The Faith of Bahá'u'lláh (the Glory of God), which was heralded by the Báb, His Forerunner, has come exactly as promised.

The Baha'i Faith, heralded by the Báb, and founded by Bahá'u'lláh, is one Faith, dating from the 23 May 1844.

M. N. Dhalla says of these *last days* that "Ahura Mazda will come at that time with his Holy Spirit . . . to accomplish this great work. The world-process will then come to its final consummation as ordained by him at the beginning of creation."[19]

Zoroaster, as recorded in the *Avesta* and in the *Gathas*, foresees the *Father* of humanity, the great *Shepherd* of the one fold. Dhalla writes, "As the great Shepherd, Ahura Mazda will bring back into the fold of righteousness all those persons . . . who had left his flock."[20]

The historical record of the life and teachings of Bahá'u'lláh, *God Passes By*, declares:

To Israel He [Bahá'u'lláh] was neither more nor less than the incarnation of the "Everlasting Father", the "Lord of Hosts" come down "with ten thousand saints"; to Christendom Christ returned "in the glory of the Father"; to Shí'ah Islám the return of the Imám Ḥusayn; to Sunní Islám the descent of the "Spirit of God" (Jesus Christ); to the Zoroastrians the promised Sháh-Bahrám; to the Hindus the reincarnation of Krishna; to the Buddhists the fifth Buddha.[21]

Thus Bahá'u'lláh's station of the *Father* extends to all the great religions of the past, for the *Flock* is humanity and the *Fold* is the sanctuary of His one universal Faith.

Bahá'u'lláh wrote that "*the Word which the Son [Jesus] concealed is made manifest*". He said, "*it hath been sent down in the form of the human temple.*"

The teachings of the Bahá'í Faith say:

... the Word was Himself [Bahá'u'lláh], and He Himself was the Father.

Bahá'u'lláh reminded the Christian world:

This is the day whereon the Rock [Peter] crieth out and shouteth ... saying: "Lo! the Father is come, and that which ye were promised in the Kingdom is fulfilled!"[22]

Bahá'u'lláh wrote to the religious leaders of Christendom:

O concourse of Bishops! ... He who is the Everlasting Father calleth aloud between earth and heaven. Blessed the ear that hath heard, and the eye that hath seen, and the heart that hath turned unto Him ... [23]

Bahá'u'lláh referred in many ways to the station of Christ as that of the Son and of Himself as the Father. He wrote to the leaders of Christian education:

Ponder ye, and be not of them who are veiled and fast asleep
... Bethlehem is astir with the Breeze of God. We hear her
voice saying: "O most generous Lord! ... The sweet savours
of Thy presence have quickened me, after I had melted in my
separation from Thee. Praised be Thou in that Thou has raised
the veils ..."[24]

And in direct words:

We called unto her ... "O Bethlehem! This Light hath risen in
the orient, and travelled towards the occident, until it reached
thee in the evening of its life. Tell Me then: Do the sons recognize the *Father*, and acknowledge Him, or do they deny Him,
even as the people aforetime denied Him [Jesus, the Son]?"[25]

Christ foretold, repeatedly, that He would go away, but would
return again. His meaning is now clear: the Holy Spirit which
dwelt within Him would return in another human temple or body.
He prophesied that the "Spirit of Truth" would come. Christ said
that this Comforter would explain to His own followers the meaning of His (Christ's) teachings. Jesus also prophesied in this same
chapter that when that great day came, the Promised One would
no longer speak in parables. The Books would be "unsealed" and
whatever His, Christ's, followers in that day asked, the *Father*
would explain to them.
Jesus says:

It is expedient for you that I go away: for if I go not away, the
Comforter will not come unto you;[26]

He promises in that same chapter:

And in that day ye shall ask me nothing ... Whatsoever ye
shall ask *the Father* in my name, he will give it you.[27]

And yet again:

These things have I spoken unto you in proverbs: but the time cometh, when I shall no more speak unto you in proverbs, but I shall shew you plainly of the Father.[28]

And finally, in the same chapter:

Howbeit when he, the Spirit of truth, is come, *he will guide you into all truth*: for he shall not speak of himself; but whatsoever he shall hear, that shall he speak ... *he shall take of mine, and shall shew it unto you.*[29]

Bahá'u'lláh echoed these words of Christ:

O kings of Christendom! Heard ye not the saying of Jesus, the Spirit of God, "I go away, and come again unto you"? Wherefore, then, did ye fail, when He did come again unto you in the clouds of heaven, to draw nigh unto Him, that ye might behold His face, and be of them that attained His Presence?[30]

And, of that same chapter of the New Testament, Bahá'u'lláh has written:

In another passage He saith: "When He, the Spirit of Truth, is come, He will guide you unto all truth." And yet, behold how, when He did bring the truth, ye refused to turn your faces towards Him, and persisted in disporting yourselves with your pastimes and fancies. Ye welcomed Him not, neither did ye seek His Presence, that ye might hear the verses of God from His own mouth ...[31]

In His longing to help the lovers of Christ to understand this truth, Bahá'u'lláh declared:

O concourse of Christians! ... This is the Day of God; turn ye unto Him ... Ye make mention of Me, and know Me not. Ye call upon Me, and are heedless of My Revelation. ... O people of the Gospel! They who were not in the Kingdom have now entered it, whilst We behold you, in this day, tarrying at the gate . . . Verily, He [Jesus] said: "Come ye after Me, and I will make you to become fishers of men." In this day, however, We say: "Come ye after Me, that We may make you to become quickeners of mankind." [32]

The "fishers of men" have now become the "quickeners of mankind" as the day of the *Son* gives way to the day of the *Father*. The complete oneness and inseparableness of the Missions of both the *Son* and the *Father*, of the Message of Christ with that of Bahá'u'lláh, is seen in these words of Bahá'u'lláh Himself cited in the book *The Promised Day Is Come*:

We, verily, have come for your sakes, and have borne the misfortunes of the world for your salvation. Flee ye the One Who hath sacrificed His life that ye may be quickened? . . . O followers of the Spirit [Jesus] . . . walk not in the footsteps of every divine [religious leader] that hath gone far astray . . . Open the doors of your hearts. He Who is the Spirit [Jesus], verily, standeth before them. Wherefore keep ye afar from Him Who hath purposed to draw you nigh unto a Resplendent Spot? . . . We, in truth, have opened unto you the gates of the Kingdom. Will ye bar the doors of your houses in My face? This indeed is naught but a grievous error.[33]

Could there be a more logical and acceptable explanation of the symbols the *Son* and the *Father*?

Next, let us consider that greatest of all Christian enigmas, that puzzle which has sundered and split the Faith of Christ, a riddle which has divided His followers, and has been responsible for more deaths than many wars – the Trinity.

Let us see what the teachings of Bahá'u'lláh tell us about the true meaning of the Trinity: the Father, the Son, and the Holy Ghost.

CHAPTER EIGHT

THE SECRET OF THE TRINITY

The question of the Trinity has long troubled the Christian world. The disputes and bloodshed which characterized the early centuries during which Christianity was being formulated into an official, orthodox creed, have now been replaced by intellectual warfare. This question has still not been resolved to the common satisfaction of all Christians. Because of the Trinity, the Jews accused the Christians of abandoning belief in one God. Because of the Trinity, the pagans refused to abandon their belief in many gods for a single Christian God, since this single God was, in reality, three gods, they said.

The subject of the true nature of Christ was the burning issue of the fourth century. Almost every Christian, in the churches, at home, and in the street, was debating the subject of the Trinity.

The brother of the famous Gregory of Nyassa, Basil, wrote of the Eastern capital city of Constantinople: "This city is full of mechanics and slaves who are all of them profound theologians, and preach in the shops and the streets. If you desire a man to change a piece of silver he informs you wherein the Son differs from the Father; if you ask the price of a loaf ... you are told that the Son is inferior to the Father; and if you inquire whether the bath is ready, the answer is, the Son was made out of nothing."[1]

St Augustine recognized that this doctrine of the Trinity was an obstacle to the mind. He spent fifteen years writing *De Trinitate* which he filled with analogies from life to explain the three persons in one God.

Hilary, in the year 367, wrote a document of twelve volumes in an effort to set forth clearly this doctrine of the Church. He was unsuccessful.

It has been said of this tempestuous time, that a creed was finally arrived at "After nearly four hundred years of conflict waged with anathema, excommunication and banishment, and aided by torture and poison. . ."[2]

Each faction employed "gladiators to sustain its point" and even armies were rallied to defend either one view or the other. H. G. Wells asserts in his history that "we find all the Christian communities so agitated and exasperated by tortuous and elusive arguments about the nature of God as to be largely negligent of the simpler teachings of charity, service and brotherhood that Jesus had inculcated."[3]

Tertullian wrote of the doctrine: "I believe because it is impossible."

These were days of great heresies in the Church because of the doctrine of the Trinity. Since there was no accepted doctrine which represented the united official view of the Church, it was difficult to decide who was the heretic and who was orthodox. The situation became so critical that at length the government was forced to intervene. The Emperor Constantine called a general council of the Church at Nicaea in A.D. 325. He attended the conference himself.

At that time the burning question was the true nature of Christ. Did one say, "Glory be to the Father, and to the Son, and to the Holy Ghost," or "Glory to the Father, through the Son, in the Holy Ghost"?

Athanasius and his followers were considered orthodox while Arius and his supporters were labelled heretic.

Constantine banished Arius, but later, when Arius professed to the Emperor that he believed in the Nicene Creed with subtle reservations, Constantine ordered that he be accepted back into the fold.

Athanasius refused, and was himself deprived of his office and banished. Arius died suddenly. His death was described as an act of God by the supporters of Athanasius, and as an act of poison by the Arians (supporters of Arius). Constantine himself died the following year, having been baptized by one of the Arian bishops whom he had previously banished, Eusebius, Bishop of Nicomedia and an Arian, who became the Emperor's "friend and counsellor".

There is no mention of the word *Trinity* in the New Testament. The charge made against Christ, in His Day, was that He made Himself God by saying that the Father was in Him, and that He and the Father were one. There was a duality, according to His enemies. A triune God had no part in the early belief.

It was not until the appearance of the fourth Gospel (approximately A.D. 100–110) that a third element is added: the Logos. John declares:

> In the beginning was the Word, and the Word was with God, and the Word was God.
> The same was in the beginning with God.[4]

The "Word" of John was read as "Logos" in the Greek. This word is said to be so complex in its meaning that there is no equivalent in modern language. The Stoics "had virtually made a god of Logos". Hellenized Jews looked upon the Logos as an intermediary between God and man to keep the One God pure and undefiled.

Thus the "Word" became the "Holy Ghost", and together with the Father and the Son laid the foundation for the Trinity; Father, Son, and Holy Ghost (Logos).

Theophilus, Bishop of Antioch about A.D. 160, appears to be the first of the Church Fathers to make use of the word *Trinity* when speaking of the Godhead. A history of that time says, "He does not, however, explain it according to the later usage of Father, Son, and Holy Ghost, but speaks of the Trinity of God, His Word, and His Wisdom."[5]

Toward the end of that tempestuous fourth century, the battle shifted from the exact nature of Christ and centred around the nature of the third Person of the Trinity, the Holy Ghost.

"Was the Holy Ghost on an equality with the Father and the Son, or was he the progeny of the Son? If so, as [Bishop] Gregory of Nazianzus pointed out, the Father must assume the ridiculous position of grandfather."[6]

Justin Martyr (A.D. 110–c.165), in his *First Apology,* states that at first the "name of God" was pronounced over the applicant who would be baptized. However, when baptism had become a more standardized sacramental procedure, the applicant was baptized: "In the name of the Father, the Son, and the Holy Ghost." And the three Persons, at last, were One.

The problems attendant on the meaning of this phrase, "the Father, the Son, and the Holy Ghost", opened the doors to the wars of the Trinity.

The concept of the Trinity was not a teaching of Christ. It was a doctrine of the Church which received official recognition in A.D. 325, nearly three hundred years after the Crucifixion.

At the Council of Nicaea the official definition of the doctrine of the Trinity was formed. Although later Councils also dealt with this subject, the view framed at Nicaea substantially represents the understanding of the Trinity accepted by the Catholic Church even today.

The Nicene Creed was adopted, teaching bodily Resurrection, and that the Father and the Son were One. The Creed was as follows:

> We believe in one God, the Father Almighty, maker of all things visible or invisible, and in one Lord Jesus Christ, the Son of God, begotten . . . not made, being of one essence [homoousion] with the Father . . . who for us men and our salvation came down and was made flesh, was made man, suffered, rose again the third day, ascended into heaven, and comes to judge the quick and the dead . . .[7]

This differs somewhat from the "Nicene Creed" now in use, which is a revision made in A.D. 362.

The Council of Nicaea defined and shaped the doctrine of the Trinity. But it could not resolve the inner and outer struggles which arose because of these vital points of belief, nor could it bring to an end the dispute between the Athanasian and Arian points of view.

A Christian historian relates that oftentimes during an episcopal election, or an excommunication of an important figure, the cities of Antioch, Alexandria, and Constantinople broke out into scenes of riot "that would have disgraced a revolution". Great numbers of people who were labelled "heretic" were massacred. Towns and villages were "utterly destroyed". Even the orthodox populace became divided into factions, and "fought like savages in the very churches".

It is recorded that at the time of the reinstatement of the Arian Bishop Macedonius, in Constantinople, three thousand people lost their lives in the fighting. This is reported as "considerably more than had suffered death in the whole ten years of the last pagan persecution".[8] "Probably more Christians were slaughtered by Christians in these two years", history records, "than by all the persecutions of Christians by pagans in the history of Rome".[9]

This question of the Trinity has remained unsettled for nearly two thousand years in spite of the efforts of religious leaders, scholars, and the intervention of governments.

Bahá'u'lláh, Who has come in fulfilment of the promises made in all the Holy Books to "unseal" the Scriptures, offers in His teachings a clear explanation of the meaning of the *Trinity: the Father, the Son, and the Holy Ghost.*

Christ was speaking of Bahá'u'lláh when He promised that the *Spirit of Truth* would come to lead men unto all truth. Christ added:

> . . . he shall not speak of himself; but whatsoever he shall hear [of God], that shall he speak . . . he shall take of mine, and shall shew it unto you.[10]

The Writings of the Bahá'í Faith explain that, in one respect, each of the great religions has a Trinity. It is found in Hinduism, Judaism, Zoroastrianism, Buddhism, Christianity, Islám, and the Bahá'í Faith. However, this Trinity is merely the *outward symbol* of an *inward truth*. It should never be interpreted as meaning that God can be defined, divided, or limited in any way.

God is One, single, unknowable, indefinable, indivisible, and infinite, Bahá'u'lláh tells us. There is no exception to this truth.

The Trinity is to be understood in the following manner: in every revealed religion there are three essential actors, (1) *the Giver*, (2) *the Gift*, and (3) *the Receiver of the Gift*.

Almighty God is *the Giver*. The *Messenger of God* is *the Receiver of the Gift*. The *Holy Spirit* is *the Gift*.

In the case of *Judaism*, *God* was the *Giver*, *Moses* the *Receiver of the Gift*, and the *Holy Spirit* revealed in the symbol of the *Burning Bush* was the *Gift*. In the case of Christianity, God, Christ, and the Holy Spirit in the symbol of the Dove. This Trinity composed of God, the Messenger, and the Holy Spirit, has existed in each of the great religions. For example:

1. God, Moses, the Burning Bush.
2. God, Zoroaster, the Sacred Fire.
3. God, Christ, the Dove.
4. God, Muhammad, the Angel Gabriel.
5. God, Bahá'u'lláh, the Holy Maiden.[11]

These are all the *outward symbol* of the same *inward truth*. They represent the moment when the Holy Spirit or Wisdom of God became directly associated with the One Who was to be His Messenger.

Bahá'u'lláh writes that God is exalted far above the knowledge of man. He cannot be described, let alone measured or divided. Therefore, there can be no trinity other than in symbol. Bahá'u'lláh says:

Regard thou the one true God as One Who is apart from, and immeasurably exalted above, all created things. The whole universe reflecteth His glory, while He is Himself independent of, and transcendeth His creatures. This is the true meaning of Divine Unity . . . He is a true believer in Divine Unity who, far from confusing duality with oneness, refuseth to allow any notion of multiplicity to becloud his conception of the singleness of God, who will regard the Divine Being as One Who, by His very nature, transcendeth the limitations of numbers.[12]

Having recognized the inviolable oneness of God, the figurative meaning of the Trinity can be understood without transgressing the fundamental principle. An analogy may help to illustrate:

There is a trinity in the *sun*, the *rays* of the sun, and the *earth*. Here too, we have the giver (sun), the gift (rays of the sun), and the receiver of the gift (earth). The sun and the earth are entirely separate and different. Yet, the source of all life on earth is from the sun, through its rays. In like manner, the source of all spiritual life on earth (the receiver of the gift) is from the Sun of Truth, God (the Giver), through His Messengers or Rays (the Gift).

The Trinity, in this case, is (1) God, *the Giver* (sun), (2) the Holy Spirit or Messenger of God, *the Gift* (rays of the sun), and (3) the people of the earth, *the receiver of the Gift* (earth). The oneness, the infinite singleness of God (the sun) is never questioned.

The sun remains completely separate and distinct from the earth, although the life-creating qualities of its rays are the source of all earthly life, including that of mankind itself.

The Writings of the Bahá'í Faith say:

> The descent of that Lordly Reality [God] into conditions and degrees would be equivalent to imperfection and contrary to perfection, and is therefore absolutely impossible . . . God is pure perfection, and creatures are but imperfections. For God to descend into the conditions of existence would be the greatest of imperfections . . . [13]

Division is not a property of God, it is a property of creation. God, the Unknowable, is now, has ever been, and will always be beyond the definition and understanding of finite man. All that we know of the attributes and qualities of God is what we see reflected in the lives of His Messengers. This is the true meaning of the Trinity.

Thus the analogy of the mirror is used in Bahá'u'lláh's teachings to demonstrate this inward truth.

God is the sun, Christ is the mirror. The Holy Spirit is the reflection of the Sun which shines in that Mirror. God is the *Giver,* Christ the *Receiver,* and the Holy Spirit is the *Gift,* The sun is the giver, the mirror the receiver, and the reflection of the sun is the gift. This same Trinity has existed in each of the great religions, and has nothing to do with the oneness of God. Nor does it in any way challenge His infinity or singleness.

When the sun is perfectly reflected in the mirror, we can see its light and feel its heat. Yet, we would never say that the sun was physically in the mirror, nor that the mirror and sun were one and the same thing. The sun remains in the heaven, and is merely reflected in the mirror.

To conclude, the teachings of the Bahá'í Faith say:

The epitome of the discourse is that the Reality of Christ was a clear mirror, and the Sun of Reality, that is to say the Essence of Oneness [God], with its infinite perfections and attributes, became visible in the mirror. The meaning is not that the Sun, which is the Essence of the Divinity, became divided and multiplied; for the Sun is one, but it appeared in the mirror. This is why Christ said, "The Father is in the Son," meaning that the Sun is visible and manifest in this mirror . . .

The Holy Spirit is the Bounty of God which becomes visible and evident in the Reality [or mirror] of Christ . . . Hence it has become certain and proved that the Essence of Divinity is absolutely unique, and has no equal, no likeness, no equivalent.

This is the signification of the Three Persons of the Trinity. If it were otherwise, the foundations of the Religion of God would rest upon an illogical proposition which the mind could never conceive, and how can the mind be forced to believe a thing which it cannot conceive? A thing cannot be grasped by the intelligence except when it is clothed with an intelligible form; otherwise it is but an effort of the imagination.

It has now become clear, from this explanation, what is the

meaning of the Three Persons of the Trinity. The Oneness of God is also proved.[14]

What tragedies have occurred because man elevates the *outward symbol* to the place of honour rightfully belonging to the *inward truth* – four hundred years of bitter physical struggle, and nearly two thousand years of verbal warfare. The Council of Nicaea (A.D. 325) declared Arius a heretic and that Christ was truly God, and that He was coequal and coeternal with the Father; and although separate, the Two were One.

The *Council of Constantinople* (A.D. 381) declared the views of Apollinarius heretical, and confirmed the Nicene Creed that Christ was God, but truly man. The *Council of Ephesus* (A.D. 431) proclaimed Nestorius a heretic, and re-emphasized the truth that the two natures of Christ and God were indivisibly one. The *Council of Chalcedon* (A.D. 451) affirmed that Christ and God were nevertheless perfectly separated and distinct.

By the end of the fourth century, the clash over the meaning of the Trinity had spread even beyond Gaul. Hilary, Bishop of Poiters (A.D. 361), vigorously defended the Nicene Creed. It is said that in his struggle "to explain the trinity," Hilary wrote a treatise consisting of twelve books.

The misunderstanding of the meaning of the Trinity led to more bloodshed among fellow Christians than all the persecutions by non-Christians. Gibbon has placed at less than two thousand the number of Christians who were executed by judicial sentence during the terrible persecutions of Diocletian and Galerius in A.D. 303–311.

It has been estimated by H. W. Smith that "the figure (2,000) would be scarcely more than doubled for the whole period of the Roman Empire – not one ten thousandth of the blood that Christianity itself was to spill in the course of its career."[15]

The persecution of Christian by Christian, for heresy in one form or another, continued for over a thousand years. Durant, in his *Age of Faith,* writes, "Compared with the persecutions of heresy in Europe from 1127 to 1492, the persecution of Christians by

Romans in the first three centuries after Christ was a mild human procedure."[16]

When Constantius, the son of the baptized Constantine, came to power, he was the "first Christian-bred emperor". He ignored his father's policy, and agreed to the Christians' request that he close the pagan temples; whoever opposed the decree would be put to death. Thus, less than fifty years after the last pagan persecution of the Christians the first Christian persecution of the pagans took place. All because of the failure to understand the true purpose and meaning of Christ's teachings.

Bahá'u'lláh declared that it was to release the "necks of men" from the chains of such cruel beliefs that He had come with His message of unity for this day.

Bahá'u'lláh writes, in His Tablet the *Glad Tidings,* that the "first Glad Tidings" which He has brought to all the people of the world "is the abolishing of the decree of religious warfare from the Book" of God.

In unsealing the truth of the meanings hidden in Scripture, Bahá'u'lláh writes in praise of God, with His own Pen:

> He is the Declarer, the Knower, the Omniscient . . . it has been our aim that the ears of the people of the world should be purified through the kawthar [river] of divine utterance from false narrations and be prepared to hearken unto the blessed, pure, exalted Word which hath appeared from the treasury of the knowledge of the Maker of heaven and Creator of names.
>
> Blessed are those who are just![17]

CHAPTER NINE

MIRACLES

Mankind in every age, including the present, shows a great taste for wonders, signs, portents, and miracles. His love of "magic" never vanishes. Although the credulity of the early centuries of this era has now been replaced by a universal scepticism, underneath there still remains a remarkable, an almost incurable demand for the miraculous.

Miracles are a drug that temporarily astonishes and influences the beholders, but a drug that soon wears off, leaving apathy and disillusionment. It creates an appetite that must be continuously fed with new miracles in order to keep it satisfied. Eventually, the miracle-lover becomes an addict whose mind can be reached by neither reason nor logic.

Christ healed ten lepers, but only one remained to acknowledge the wonder and to thank him. Christ asked:

> Were there not ten cleansed? But where are the nine?
> There are not found that returned to give glory to God, save this stranger.[1]

Christ Himself forcefully demonstrated the need for man to believe because of the teachings He had brought, and not because of miracles. When Thomas refused to believe without the proof of a wonder, Jesus rebuked him, saying:

> Thomas, because thou hast seen me, thou hast believed: blessed are they that have not seen, and yet have believed.[2]

Of Christ it is also written that for many others, the miracles had
no meaning:

> But though he had done so many miracles before them, yet
> they believed not on him.[3]

Bahá'u'lláh strongly denounced this hunger for miracles. He said
to the religious leaders of Baghdad who demanded a *sign* for the
proof of His Mission:

> . . . The Cause of God is not a theatrical display that is pre-
> sented every hour, of which some new diversion may be asked
> for every day. If it were thus, the Cause of God would become
> mere child's play.[4]

Religious history shows clearly that miracles have never been the
means of changing the hearts of men. Miracles may astonish, may
please the onlooker, but they are soon forgotten. The purpose of the
Messenger of God is to transform the character of mankind. His
Mission is to draw people nearer to God through their own inner
volition, not by His outward compulsion. A man's belief in God and
religion must be the result of understanding, not mystification.

The Writings of the Bahá'í Faith explain that the primary reason
for the appearance of a Messenger of God is:

> . . . to educate the souls of men, and refine the character of
> every living man . . . The most vital duty, in this day, is to
> purify your characters, to correct your manners, and improve
> your conduct.[5]

The teachings of the Bahá'í Faith insist that its followers:

> . . . must show forth such character and conduct among His
> [God's] creatures, that the fragrance of their holiness may be
> shed upon the whole world, and may quicken the [spiritually]
> dead . . . [6]

This is why Moses, Christ, Bahá'u'lláh, and all the Messengers of God have come: to reform both the inner and outer life of men. They did not come to perform miracles and to work wonders.

The teachings of Bahá'u'lláh's Faith point out that the proof of a World-Educator or Messenger of God is the education which He gives to man. The proof of the great bridge-builder is the great bridge. The proof of the great singer is the great song. One cannot establish a reputation as a great architect by changing wine into water, or a stick into a snake. Only a great building, built according to his specifications, can prove that a man is a great architect. In like manner, miracles do not prove the validity of a Messenger of God. His Message proves it. Miracles are only secondary proofs. Most frequently such miracles are of a symbolical nature, and should not be taken literally.

The Writings of the Bahá'í Faith say:

> What, then, is the mission of the divine Prophets? Their mission is the education and advancement of the world of humanity. They are the real Teachers and Educators, the universal Instructors of mankind. If we wish to discover whether any of these great Souls or Messengers was in reality a Prophet of God, we must investigate the facts surrounding His life and history, and the first point of our investigation will be the education He bestowed upon mankind. If He has been an Educator, if He has really trained a nation or a people, causing it to rise from the lowest depths of ignorance to the highest station of knowledge, then we are sure that He was a Prophet. This is a plain and clear method of procedure, proof that is irrefutable . . . We do not need to mention miracles, saying that out of rock water gushed forth, for such miracles and statements may be denied and refused by those who hear them. The *deeds* of Moses are conclusive evidences of His Prophethood.[7]

The same is true of Christ, Muhammad, Buddha, Krishna, Zoroaster, or Bahá'u'lláh. That They are Educators is proved by Their teachings. That They can attract the hearts of men is proved by the great number of Their followers. Their Messages are the proof of the validity of Their Missions. This is the real miracle: that they bring a knowledge which banishes ignorance.

After all, man is surrounded every day by so-called miracles. Often he is entirely unaware of them. If a handful of steel screws is dropped, they fall to the floor, drawn by gravity. Yet, if a powerful magnet or electromagnet approaches them, they fly upward, breaking this natural law of gravitation. A higher power has been applied. In an earlier age this would have been considered an astounding miracle. All wonders that appear to be contrary to known laws seem to be miracles.

It is a miracle that man flies like a bird in his jet planes; dives in the sea like a fish in his submarines; races across the land at terrific speeds; imprisons light in a glass bulb; speaks in an instant across continents; witnesses on a television screen events taking place at that moment thousands of miles away; sustains the animation of the heart artificially so that vital surgery may be performed; or replaces a blind eye with one that sees. We are encircled with miracles every moment of our lives.

The ink from the typewriter, by which this chapter is being written, is composed of countless, immeasurable atoms. Each one is a solar system with its own central star and planets circling around it in the form of electrons.

In the space of time it takes to type this page, each electron racing around the central proton, as the planets circle our sun, will have travelled much farther than the distance from New York to London and return.

The physical wonders that encompass us stagger the mind. How can we hope to take in the spiritual reality that underlies them? These miracles do not break the law of God's natural creation. They are truths that have always existed, but have remained until recently hidden in the vast treasure-house of God's knowledge. At last, the developing mind of man has brought them out from the unknown into the known.

Explaining the proton, electron, atom, or molecule to a person living in the day of Moses or Christ would have been impossible. To accept such fantastic "miracles" would have been equally impossible for them. Yet we accept these truths now as a part of our everyday life. Is it any wonder that Jesus said to Nicodemus:

If I have told you earthly things, and ye believe not, how shall ye believe, if I tell you of heavenly things?[8]

The proof of the Messenger of God is His Message and never His miracles. When a man wishes to purchase an automobile, he accepts or rejects it depending upon the performance of that car. He judges it according to the qualities which an automobile is supposed to possess. He does not buy the car because the salesman is able to change tyres into golden platters.

This truth applies in all fields. A dog is not measured by his ability to pull like a horse, nor is a horse judged by his bark, eyesight, sense of smell, and instinct for watchfulness and protection. The end must partake of the means. If the end is education, the means must be instruction. If one wishes to obtain a teaching degree, he goes to school, not to a wizard, a sorcerer, or a magician.

Bahá'u'lláh has plainly written that the Messengers of God have come to educate the minds and souls of men, to uplift their station and dignity. They have not come to blunt men's senses or dull their minds with miracles. Bahá'u'lláh's Writings say:

It is incumbent upon every man, in this Day, to hold fast unto whatsoever will promote the interests, and exalt the station, of all nations and just governments. Through each and every one of the verses which the Pen of the Most High hath revealed, the doors of love and unity have been unlocked and flung open to the face of men . . . Whatsoever hath led the children of men to shun one another, and hath caused dissensions and divisions amongst them, hath, through the revelation of these words, been nullified and abolished. From the heaven of God's will, and for the purpose of *ennobling the world of being and of elevating the minds and souls of men, hath been sent down that which is the most effective instrument for the education of the whole human race* . . . It is not his to boast who loveth his country, but it is his who loveth the world. Through the power released by these exalted words He hath lent a fresh impulse, and set a new direction, to the birds of men's hearts, *and hath obliterated every trace of . . . limitation from God's holy Book.*[9] (Author's italics)

Yet, despite the fact that religion is primarily a progressive system of spiritual education, the cry of man has ever been that recorded in the Bible:

. . . if the Lord be with us, why then is all this befallen us? and where be all his miracles . . .?[10]

Miracles, wonder, and magic create an insatiable thirst among men. Each wonder must be eclipsed by a greater marvel. Eventually all bonds of restraint are gone, and miracles become, not the property of the Prophet, but of His disciples and apostles. Next they become the daily food and drink of the populace. The Church made this alarming discovery itself, and finally had to place an iron hand on the working of miracles, as well as on the reporting of such miracles.

An historian has written of the appalling results of the love of miracles in the Christian Faith:

A multitude of mysterious and supernatural beings had descended into Christianity from pagan antiquity, and were still coming into it from Germany, Scandinavia, and Ireland, as trolls, elves, giants, fairies, goblins, gnomes, ogres, banshees, mysterious dragons, blood-sucking vampires; and new superstitions were always entering Europe from the East. Dead men walked the air as hosts; men who had sold themselves to the Devil roamed woods and fields as werewolves; the souls of children dead before baptism haunted the marshes as will-o'-the-wisps. When St Edmund Rich saw a flock of black crows he recognized them at once as a flock of devils come to fetch the soul of a local usurer. When a demon is exorcised from a man, said many a medieval story, a big black fly – sometimes a dog – could be seen issuing from his mouth. The population of devils never declined.[11]

There were, of course, good angels who were looked upon with favour, if kept under reasonable control. This idea of a special angel to protect each child and adult came from Zoroastrian theology, not Christian, though it was not a teaching of Zoroaster. Dawson, in his *Ethical Religion of Zoroaster,* tells of "guardian angels" for every man, woman and child. As Durant states, "The majestic monotheism of the founder became – as in Christianity – the polytheism of the people."

The Church struggled against these beliefs in miraculous events. She punished severely. She tried to root out black magic and other illegal wonders. In spite of this effort, magic and miracles "flourished in a thousand places . . . nearly everybody believed in some magical means of turning the power of supernatural beings to a desired end."[12]

Iacopo de Voragine, Archbishop of Genoa, wrote a book in which he had a magical story for each day of the year, a story about the miracles of one of the Saints, including the slaying of dragons. Although the Church "counselled a certain suspension of belief" concerning some of these stories, it was fruitless. The stories were loved, believed, and accepted.

One account states that "The enlightened Agobard, Archbishop of Lyons in the ninth century, complained that 'things of such absurdity are believed by Christians as no one ever aforetime could induce the heathen to believe.'"[13]

Miracles which had once been used to inspire, now served only to degrade. It was too late to stop it. Pandora had opened the box herself.

Bahá'u'lláh recognized the danger of miracles. He knew the insecurity of any heart which insisted upon miracles before "believing". Bahá'u'lláh courageously challenged this demand for

87

miracles. His words have put an end to any religious importance which might be attributed to miracles. Bahá'u'lláh spoke on behalf of all the Messengers of God, for all time.

While He was in exile in Baghdad, near the place along the river Chebar where Ezekiel in vision had seen *the glory of God,* Bahá'u'lláh was under attack by the religious leaders of the area. They had devised a cunning plan by which they could arouse the animosity of the people against Bahá'u'lláh: miracles.

Their plan was to belittle Bahá'u'lláh in the eyes of the people. These religious leaders sent an emissary named Ḥasan-i-'Ammú to Bahá'u'lláh with a list of abstruse questions taken from vague and fragmentary references found in their Scripture and Traditions. They felt that Bahá'u'lláh would surely make a fool of Himself in trying to answer such difficult questions. As no priest or scholar among their own most illustrious leaders had yet been able to resolve these problems, how could Bahá'u'lláh ever hope to? They chuckled with glee at the prospect of His humiliation.

Bahá'u'lláh, Who had come to *unseal* the meaning of the holy Books of the past, answered the questions briefly and lucidly. He answered each question to the complete satisfaction, as well as the utter amazement, of the representative of the religious leaders. It was not a matter of "miracles", but a matter of knowledge.

These religious leaders were forced to recognize the vastness of Bahá'u'lláh's knowledge. But they would not be shaken from their purpose. Bahá'u'lláh must be discredited at any cost. Therefore they continued with their conspiracy. They decided to appeal to Bahá'u'lláh for a wonder, a sign, for a physical miracle.

"We are not contented," they said, "we are not convinced by this [His great knowledge]. We do not acknowledge the validity of his [Bahá'u'lláh's] mission just because he is wise and righteous. Therefore we ask him to show us a miracle in order to satisfy and tranquillize our hearts."

The emissary they sent to Bahá'u'lláh repeated these words. He said, "We testify that the knowledge thou dost possess is such as none can rival. Such a knowledge however, is insufficient proof to vindicate the exalted station which the people ascribe to thee."

It was the same old familiar cry to which Christ had listened: "It is not enough that men love you, follow you, and that your words and teachings are acknowledged to be true and beautiful. We would see a *sign* from you."

Ḥasan-i-'Ammú said to Bahá'u'lláh, "Produce if thou speakest the truth, what the combined forces of the peoples of the earth are powerless to produce."

To the surprise of Ḥasan-i-'Ammú, the representative of the religious leaders, Bahá'u'lláh agreed at once to perform such a miracle. This was a step unique in the annals of religious history: a Messenger of God agreeing beforehand to perform a miracle, at the request of the religious leaders, to test their sincerity. Bahá'u'lláh announced to the emissary that He would happily perform a suitable miracle. No doubt His inner eye twinkled with amusement as He contemplated the outcome.

"Although you have no right to ask this," Bahá'u'lláh told the emissary, ". . . still I allow and accept this request."

Bahá'u'lláh, knowing that the real purpose behind the request was to humiliate Him publicly and thus prove Him to be false, insisted upon certain conditions.

"The 'ulamás [religious leaders] must assemble, and, with one accord, choose one miracle." This was Bahá'u'lláh's first demand. There was yet another condition. They must also agree, He said, to put in writing that "after the performance of this miracle they will no longer entertain doubts about Me, and that all will acknowledge and confess the truth of My Cause".

Bahá'u'lláh was not to be betrayed by their cunning. He told their representative that it was not enough for them merely to agree to put this in writing, they must actually sign such a document before the performance of the agreed-upon miracle.

"Let them seal this paper", He told the emissary, "and bring it to Me. This must be the accepted criterion: if the miracle is performed, no doubt will remain for them and if not, We shall be convicted of imposture."

This was a clear, courageous reply. The challenge had been accepted by Bahá'u'lláh and thrown back to the religious leaders.

Ḥasan-i-ʿAmmú, the representative, was deeply affected both by Baháʾuʾlláh's answers to his abstruse theological questions, and by the generosity and willingness of Baháʾuʾlláh to perform the miracle.

"There is no more to be said," Ḥasan-i-ʿAmmú declared.

He arose from his interview, expressed his new-found respect and admiration for Baháʾuʾlláh, and departed to deliver Baháʾuʾlláh's challenging reply to the clergy.[14]

"Days passed and he failed to come back to Us," Baháʾuʾlláh recorded. "Eventually, there came another messenger who informed Us that the people [leaders] had given up what they originally had purposed."[15]

The original emissary sent word to Baháʾuʾlláh that the august body of religious leaders had failed to arrive at a decision. They had been stunned by Baháʾuʾlláh's challenge. They could not agree upon a miracle for Baháʾuʾlláh to perform. They could not now even agree upon the wisdom of letting Baháʾuʾlláh attempt to perform a miracle of any kind. They had expected an outright refusal from Baháʾuʾlláh. They had planned to use this refusal to denounce Him as a fraud. Now they were deeply concerned about the danger of giving Baháʾuʾlláh any opportunity to perform a miracle; even if they were ever able to agree upon one definite miracle. They decided that it would be safer to drop the matter entirely. They were interested in a victory over Baháʾuʾlláh that would debase Him, not in offering Him an opportunity to exalt Himself at their expense. These religious leaders could not find any satisfactory answer to the troublesome question they kept asking themselves: "What if Baháʾuʾlláh should actually *perform* the miracle?"

The news of their challenge to Baháʾuʾlláh, and of His bold reply, was given widespread publicity. The original emissary, Ḥasan-i-ʿAmmú, made the story everywhere known. He travelled to Persia, and while in Tehran, told the story in person to the Foreign Minister.[16]

When Baháʾuʾlláh was informed of the decision of the religious leaders in reply to His offer, He said: "We have through this all-satisfying, all-embracing message which We sent, revealed and vindicated the miracles of all the Prophets, inasmuch as We left the choice to the 'ulamás [clergy] themselves, undertaking to reveal whatever they would decide upon."[17]

In speaking of His offer to perform this miracle in Baghdad, Bahá'u'lláh said once again that these *outer* wonders were of no importance. It was the *inner* spiritual truths which the Messengers of God taught that were everything. The experience of every Prophet, Bahá'u'lláh said, had been the same:

> Whoso hath in bygone ages asked Us [the Messengers of God] to produce the signs of God, hath, no sooner We revealed them to him, repudiated God's truth. The people, however, have, for the most part, remained heedless. They whose eyes are illumined with the light of understanding . . . will embrace His truth. These are they who are truly sincere.[18]

Eyes that are opened to the *inner* light will see and believe. *This* is the real miracle. It is this *inner* conviction, not an outer compulsion, that makes a true and lasting believer in any truth, religious or otherwise. Jesus explained this principle to His disciples when He said:

> Ye seek me, not because ye saw the miracles, but because ye did eat of the loaves, and were filled.[19]

Christ, in these words, states two truths:

1. It is not the miracles, but the inward truth that nourishes.
2. Many miracles, such as the miracle of the loaves and fishes, are symbolical in their meaning.

The story of the five barley loaves and two small fishes which fed five thousand has been considered by some to be one of the greatest of Christ's miracles. Yet Christ Himself made it plain that it was not a physical, but a symbolical marvel. Christ fed the people with what he called "the meat which perishes not, the meat that is everlasting". He fed them the "bread of life" which He said was the teaching of the Messenger of God who had come down from heaven to give life to the world. Christ did not refer to the "loaves and fishes" as an *outward* wonder at all. When He spoke to His disciples of this event, He said: "Ye seek me, *not* because ye saw the miracles, but because ye did *eat of the loaves and were filled.*" Miracles and partaking of the "bread of life" were two different things.

The Bahá'í teaching on miracles is expressed by 'Abdu'l-Bahá as follows:

> . . . for the Manifestations these miracles and wonderful signs have no importance. They do not even wish to mention them. For if we consider miracles a great proof, they are still only proofs and arguments for those who are present when they are performed. . . . The meaning is not that the Manifestations are unable to perform miracles, for they have all power. But for them inner sight, spiritual healing and eternal life are the valuable and important things.[20]

If miracles are ascribed to the founders of religion, and become engrafted upon the teaching, they will inevitably be used to mislead, delude, and defraud the simple and trusting among the children of men, says 'Abdu'l-Bahá. History clearly illustrates this.

Thus it is imperative that men should understand the symbolical *inward* truth behind these *outward* stories, mysteries, and ceremonies which are found in all the past religions in varying degrees. Otherwise the sincere soul will become disillusioned when he learns that all these miracles he has held so dear, and considered as the exclusive and sacred property of his own belief, were loved with equal devotion by equally sincere souls in the pagan past. The great rival of Christianity in the early centuries, Mithraism, is an example.

The ceremony in the Mithraeum (natural cave or vault) was more crude and less sublimated than Christian worship, but greatly similar with its seven degrees of Mithraic mysteries, "one involving a communion of bread and wine, another a purification of the hands and tongue with honey, the third a simulated death and resurrection, and in a fourth the subject was marked on the forehead with a symbolic sign. Mystic rituals such as the repetition of sacred formulas, the chanting of music, and the purification by baptism, by the ringing of bells, by the sacred fire of the temple candles . . . The highest degree was held by the priests who were addressed as 'pater', a name later corrupted to 'papa' and then to 'pope.'"[21]

"The term *papa*, 'father', which became in English *pope,* was applied in the three centuries to any Christian bishop."[22]

Paganism was keenly aware of the power of an appeal to the physical senses, as were Judaism, Zoroastrianism, Buddhism, and the ancient faiths, in varying forms. With their altars, rituals, robes, and candles they appealed powerfully to the sense of sight. Incense and perfumes appealed to the sense of smell; bells, chanting and singing to the sense of hearing; the bread and wine to the sense of taste; and beads and sacred objects to the sense of touch.

The early Church followed this example, and improved upon it. It established a magnificent pageantry of powerful appeal to all the physical senses. This accounted for, and still accounts for, the grave difficulty which its followers had and have in objectively seeing and understanding the true meaning behind these symbolical ceremonies. These rituals became the thing believed in, instead of the vital truths which they symbolized; just as the miracles became the source of Christ's greatness to many, rather than the spiritual truths for which they stood.

This dilemma has been satirically expressed by a biographer of George Santayana who observed: "So powerful was the hold of church ritual and pageantry upon him that he, Santayana, was described as one who believed that there was no God, and that the Virgin Mary was His mother."

If the greatness of Christ were to be based upon His performing miracles, then it would lower rather than raise His station. Such miracles were not performed by Christ alone. Others besides Christ had performed these same wonders, according to written

record, and many, many years before Christianity. Pagan literature is filled with stories of such miracles as the *loaves and fishes,
walking on water, raising from the dead, restoring sight and hearing,
casting out devils,* and *resurrection.* It is obvious that these miracles
did not originate with Christianity. There are many accounts of
such events. One of them will suffice:

> Jesus turned water into wine, as did Dionysus on January sixth
> of every year; and multiplied loaves of bread, as did Elisha. He
> walked on water like Orion, Poseidon's son. He raised men
> from the dead, as did Elijah and Elisha – this feat had once
> been so common that Aristophanes, in *The Frogs (ca.* 405 B.C.),
> made Dionysius say of Hermes and of Hermes' father that per-
> forming resurrections was a family profession. He [Christ] gave
> sight to the blind by application of his spittle, the remedy which
> Thoth had used to restore the eye of Horus . . . He healed the
> leper, the lunatic, the deaf and dumb, as did Asklepios.[23]

Bahá'u'lláh wrote of the miracles which are attributed to Christ. He
assigns to them their true worth and beauty. Bahá'u'lláh declares:

> We testify that when He [Christ] came into the world, He shed
> the splendour of His glory upon all created things. Through
> Him the leper recovered from the leprosy of perversity and
> ignorance. Through Him, the unchaste and wayward were
> healed. Through His power, born of Almighty God, the eyes of
> the blind were opened, and the soul of the sinner sanctified.
>
> Leprosy may be interpreted as any veil that interveneth
> between man and the recognition of the Lord, his God. Whoso
> alloweth himself to be shut out from Him is indeed a leper, who
> shall not be remembered in the Kingdom of God, the Mighty,
> the All-Praised. We bear witness that through the power of
> the *Word of God* every leper was cleansed, every sickness was
> healed, every human infirmity was banished. He [Christ] it is
> Who purified the world. Blessed is the man who, with a face
> beaming with light, hath turned towards Him.[24]

In these words, we see yet another of the meanings which Bahá'u'lláh has *unsealed* from the sacred literature of the past. He has shown His strong disapproval of the use of miracles as a source of proof for the validity of the Mission of the Messenger of God. In clear, unmistakable language, Bahá'u'lláh calls upon His followers not to become a prey to outward *wonders* and *signs*. He urges them instead to look with an inward eye. He says:

> Mine aim hath ever been, and still is, to suppress whatever is the cause of contention amidst the peoples of the earth, and of separation amongst the nations, so that all men may be sanctified from every earthly attachment, and be set free to occupy themselves with their own interests. *We entreat Our loved ones not to besmirch the hem of Our raiment with the dust of falsehood, neither to allow references to what they have regarded as miracles and prodigies to debase Our rank and station, or mar the purity and sanctity of Our name.*[25]

No words could be plainer than these, regarding the station of miracles. Bahá'u'lláh warns mankind that the *"corrosion of ungodliness is eating into the vitals of human society."* Nothing, He says, but the power of the Word of God through His Messengers, can cleanse and revive it.

Then Bahá'u'lláh asks: is it possible for man to transmute base metal into gold? As perplexing and difficult as such a task may be, He informs us, the still greater task of *"converting satanic strength"* (worldly desire) into heavenly power (detachment) is a task which the Messengers of God have *"been empowered to accomplish"*. No miracle can be greater than such a wonder.

Bahá'u'lláh writes:

> The Word of God, alone, can claim the distinction of being endowed with the capacity required for so great and far-reaching a change.[26]

This, after all, Bahá'u'lláh tells us, is the real miracle: the transformation of base human clay into a spiritual being, the raising of man above his animal desires to his proper place in the human kingdom. This is indeed the greatest miracle of all. This gradual spiritual evolution of man is also the entire purpose of human existence. It is for the purpose of assisting in the performance of *this* miracle, which is one of education, that the Messengers and Prophets come to earth.

The "Word" of the Messenger of God changes the sinner into the saint. It heals the leprosy of disbelief. It opens the eyes of the spiritually blind. It restores life to those who are spiritually dead. It brings agreement and love between light and dark skins. It unites men of conflicting religious belief. It links together men of opposing nations. Without destroying the value of the individual contribution of each, it fuses into willing cooperation the active and passive personalities; the dominant and the recessive; the introvert and the extrovert. It harmonizes the views of capital and labour. It restores health and unity to crippled mortals by converting "virtuous thieves, generous backbiters, and kindly profligates" into wholesome, integrated human beings. It inspires the divergent members of society to surrender all, spontaneously and generously, even life if necessary, for their fellowmen, who may be perfect strangers.

All this is done, Bahá'u'lláh tells us, through the power of God, "the Divine Charmer". Is there any miracle that can be compared with this miracle?

CHAPTER TEN

ABOUT HEAVEN AND HELL – NOT A MATTER OF GEOGRAPHY

Bahá'u'lláh's teachings carefully explain the *inner meaning* behind these *outer symbols* of *Heaven* and *Hell,* and tell us why these symbolic terms should not be taken literally.

According to the Bahá'í Faith, Heaven is harmony with the Will of God and unity with our fellowmen: a state of perfection. Hell is the want of such harmony: a state of imperfection. Thus, a man may be either in Heaven or Hell while still living on this earth. The joys of Heaven are spiritual joys, and the pains of Hell consist of the deprivation of those joys.[1]

Heaven is a figurative way of expressing the satisfaction of knowing and loving God. Heaven is the attaining of the utmost perfection of which one is capable. Heaven is the obtaining of spiritual life. It is entering into the Kingdom of God and accepting the Messenger of God, that spiritual Educator, when He appears. This act of belief leads man closer to spiritual Truth because of his new-found knowledge; and, hence, closer to God. Heaven is the complete assurance that the vital part of man is not put into the ground at his death, and that he has the opportunity and privilege of attaining everlasting life.

Hell is the opposite of all these things. Hell is the tragedy of being deprived of the knowledge of God. Hell is the failure to acquire spiritual perfections while on this earth. Hell is the loss of spiritual station in the world to come.

Heaven is life. Hell is death. The Scriptures themselves have made this symbolical point, but man, interpreting the Scriptures literally, has too often failed to understand this truth. In Hebrew, the word Sheol (Hell) "most commonly signifies the grave, or the place or state of the dead". Sometimes[2] it refers to Hell, sometimes to the grave.

David says, in the Psalms:

Let death seize upon them, and let them go down quick into *hell*: for wickedness is in their dwellings, and among them.[3]

The alternate meaning given for Hell in this verse is grave. The "wickedness" of men has brought them *death* or *hell*, for they are far from God.

When Jonah refused to serve God and fled from Him, he was cast into the belly of the whale. This was a symbol of his temporary spiritual death, his grave, his Hell. Jonah himself laments:

. . . I cried by reason of mine affliction unto the Lord, and he heard me: out of the *belly of hell* cried I . . . [4]

The belly of *hell*, Jonah says, not the belly of the *whale*. It is clearly a symbol for the deprivation of spiritual sight.

As the doctrine of the Church grew more complicated, Heaven and Hell were no longer sufficient to resolve all of the problems which presented themselves. Purgatory and Limbo were added. Thus, *reward* and *punishment* became a matter of geography. This concept of a "purgatory" or degrees of Heaven and Hell was already popular in the theology of Zoroaster, long before Christianity. All dead souls passed over the *Sifting Bridge* and the wicked fell to a level commensurate with their sins. Dawson, in his *Ethical Religion of Zoroaster*, says that there was only temporary punishment for the soul which had more virtues than vices. If he had sinned, but had also done good works in his day, he would rise to heaven after 12,000 years.

The Hell from which the Messenger of God releases the people when He comes to teach them the Truth is the Hell of ignorance and error. He lifts the souls to the Heaven of understanding. The graves of ignorance and error give up their spiritually dead at His Word.

St John the Divine records in *Revelation* how he saw the vision of the coming of the Messiah:

> . . . and his name is called *The Word of God.*[5]

In the next chapter, he declares that when "the books were opened" or *unsealed:*

> . . . death and hell delivered up the dead which were in them . . .[6]

The Messenger of God, or the Word of God, raises the spiritually dead from the graves of error. He frees them from the Hell of unbelief in which they lie dead and imprisoned.

In almost the next breath, St John says that he saw the "new Jerusalem" which is the Word of God come down from Heaven. In that same chapter he says that the Messiah made "all things new". This new Jerusalem, or Word of God, he said, had no need of the sun (former teachings and explanations):

> . . . for *the glory of God* did lighten it. . .[7]

Bahá'u'lláh, Whose name means *the Glory of God,* has "opened the books" and clarified the symbols which have confused and divided the people of religion for centuries. He has not come to raise the spiritually dead of any single Faith, but rather to give life to the spiritually dead of every past belief, and to raise them from their tombs of misunderstanding. He has let into their tombs of death the fresh air and sunlight of truth by his wholesome explanations.

The teachings of the Bahá'í Faith explain that the references made in the past by the Messengers of God to "paradise, to hell-fire, to future reward and punishment", were made to uplift the souls of men. These conceptions of Heaven and Hell were necessary symbols for an age in which there was little or no education.

These analogies and parables of the past helped to convey an inward truth so that the people of those ages might grasp the importance of living a pure, moral, and useful life. Unfortunately, literal-minded mankind has given a permanency to these stories and symbols which is entirely unjustified.

These ancient appendages are unsuited to man's present level of spiritual growth. Man has clung to the *outward symbol* and has abandoned the *inward truth*. In a more simple age, outward physical symbol was necessary to express the meaning; but in an advanced intellectual age, the *inward truth* itself can be explained and understood.

For this reason Bahá'u'lláh has come to *unseal* these *inward truths*.

The actual pain of physical burning, such as has been described as a punishment of Hell, can only be associated with the body and its material senses. Physical pain is left behind with the death of the physical body. The hell-fire that the soul can feel is the fire of separation, the dreadful pain of being kept away from the nearness and beauty of God. This pain is likened to having an unquenchable thirst, and being deprived of the cooling waters of the love of God. This is the real Hell.

The spiritual worlds, Bahá'u'lláh tells us, are infinite. Thus, the finite mind cannot grasp them, nor describe them. Consequently, the language used in dealing with these realities, by its very nature, must be poetic and symbolic rather than exact.

The Hell of brimstone and fire was a symbol used in the religious writings of the past to convey the most dreadful terrors imaginable which awaited those who disobeyed the laws of God, or who lived in a manner contrary to the spiritual life. The Heaven of pearly gates, roads of precious gems, with golden stairs, was likewise a symbol of the richness of the reward awaiting those faithful souls who lived in accordance with the Will of God.

These old-fashioned material symbols of Heaven and Hell were used to convey an *inward truth* which could not otherwise have been understood at the time. Mankind has now outgrown them. The human mind has become more mature. Man is at last able to understand that the true rewards and punishments are spiritual and intellectual, not physical. He is able to realize that there is no pain which can equal the anguish of a soul which has neglected or deprived itself of its opportunities in this life. Physical suffering can never compare with the sorrows of the spirit. Almost every man knows that the greatest hardship he can be made to suffer is to be weighed down with an inner sorrow or grief. This anguish can become so great that he will even seek to destroy his physical being in an effort to escape it.

In this day man does not need an outward symbol to portray the terrors of Hell. This Hell exists within him when he shuts himself out from God, from service to mankind, from justice, from right doing. No Hell, Bahá'u'lláh's teachings say, can compare with the agony which such a soul feels upon leaving this world.

"Hell is an extinct volcano," as far as its physical nature is concerned. The day of the so-called Devil, with the long tail, horns, and spear, is gone. There is no fiery furnace with such a personified evil character in charge.

Heaven and Hell are spiritual conditions, not actual places. Heaven and Hell are not a matter of geography. Closeness to God is Heaven, remoteness from Him is Hell. Perfections of the spirit are Heaven, imperfections Hell. To have a good and praiseworthy human character is Heaven, to have an animal nature is Hell. A full, rich life of love and service to mankind keeps a man in Heaven, while an empty life of hatred, prejudice, greed and opposition keeps him in Hell. It is that simple.

Pleasure and pain, light and dark, joy and sorrow, are all attempts to express the inexpressible Heaven and Hell. They can only be described or understood as conditions: one of complete fulfilment, one of utter emptiness. It is impossible to catch the ocean in a cup, and all words used in an effort to explain these subjects must walk blind and crippled toward their unattainable goal. The Writings of the Bahá'í Faith say:

> . . . we must endeavour with heart and soul in order that the veil covering the eye of inner vision may be removed, that we

may . . . realize that material blessings as compared with spiritual bounties are as nothing.[8]

They are Hell as compared with Heaven. And in another place:

> In the matrix of the mother we were the recipients of endowments and blessings of God, yet these were as nothing compared to the powers and graces bestowed upon us after birth into this human world. Likewise, if we are born from the matrix of this physical and phenomenal environment into the freedom and loftiness of the spiritual life and vision, we shall consider this mortal existence and its blessings as worthless by comparison.[9]

It is the difference between the grave and life, between Hell and Heaven. And, finally:

> Verily, the Pen is unable to move in a befitting manner in explaining this truth, its exaltation and loftiness. The Hand of Mercy shall cause it to enter men's minds, though it can never be grasped by an explanation, nor be described by those means which are available to the world.[10]

> As to those that have tasted of the fruit of man's earthly existence, which is the recognition of the one true God, exalted be His glory, their life hereafter is such as We are unable to describe. The knowledge thereof is with God, alone, the Lord of all worlds.[11]

These are a few glimpses into the true meaning of the symbols *Heaven* and *Hell* as *unsealed* by the Pen of Bahá'u'lláh from the sacred Books of the past.

CHAPTER ELEVEN

WHEN THE STARS FELL FROM HEAVEN

What does it mean in the Scriptures when it says: "The stars shall fall from heaven"? What is the explanation of the words: "The sun and the moon shall be darkened"?

Bahá'u'lláh has *unsealed* the meaning of these puzzling statements in His *Book of Certitude.*

These strange, and apparently impossible, events were foretold in even the oldest sacred books. Such prophecies have caused men to turn away from the Messengers of God in every age.

The people of Christ's day rejected Him because they had not witnessed the fulfilment of the signs which were to foretell the coming of their Messiah. The Christians reject Bahá'u'lláh for the same reason. The Christians and the Jews are both awaiting the same sign: the fall of the stars from Heaven. They are still awaiting the physical appearance of signs and wonders which have already been fulfilled spiritually and symbolically.

Bahá'u'lláh explains in His Writings that these signs were actually fulfilled at the time of Christ for the Jews, and have been fulfilled again in this day for the Christians.

Unfortunately, religion, which in its youthful vitality and purity is able to open man's inward eye to these spiritual truths, gradually loses this inner strength. The spiritual truths become obscured or forgotten while the symbols which represent them, the rites and rituals, become the all-important thing.

The people in every age, blindly following their leaders, deny the new Messenger of God in much the same manner as the people of a previous age had denied the Messenger who had appeared to them. The believers in the old religion refuse to accept either the new Messenger or His teachings, in spite of the fact that His true purpose in coming is to restore the original vitality of their own Faith and to heal their ills and resolve their problems.

Bahá'u'lláh says of the people who live in the day of the appearance of any Messenger of God:

> Had they sought with a humble mind from the Manifestations [Messengers] of God in every Dispensation the true meaning of these words revealed in the sacred books – words the misapprehension of which hath caused men to be deprived of the recognition [of the Prophet] – they surely would have been guided to the light of the Sun of Truth, and would have discovered the mysteries of divine knowledge and wisdom.[1]

In order to prevent such a misunderstanding in this present day, Bahá'u'lláh says:

> This servant will now share with thee a dewdrop out of the fathomless ocean of the truths treasured in these holy words . . .[2]

His purpose, Bahá'u'lláh states, is to clarify the allusions and symbolical language of Scripture so that man will henceforth be prevented from denying the Messenger of God because of misunderstanding.

One of the prophecies which has kept the Jews, Christians, and Muslims from accepting the Promised One concerns the signs that will appear in the heavens at the time of His appearance. One after another the followers of each of these religions have insisted that none of these signs has ever been fulfilled. Among these prophecies is this often-quoted one from the book of *Joel:*

> The sun shall be turned into darkness, and the moon into blood, before the great and the terrible day of the Lord come.
> For behold, in those days . . . I will also gather all nations . .

. the sun and the moon shall be dark, and the stars shall with-draw their shining.[3]

This same prophecy is to be found also in the Books of *Isaiah, Ezekiel,* and *Daniel* and others. The maintaining that this prophecy was to be fulfilled only in the day of Christ is proved to be false by the number of times it is repeated in the New Testament in *Matthew, Luke* and *Revelation.*

Christ Himself foretells these same events which will take place in the day of His return:

> Immediately after the tribulation of those days shall the sun be darkened, and the moon shall not give her light, and the stars shall fall from heaven, and the powers of the heavens shall be shaken . . . and they shall see the Son of man coming in the clouds of heaven with power and great glory.[4]

It is equally clear that the prophecy concerning the "assembling of the nations" associated with these signs in the heavens did not refer to the day of Jesus, for Christ Himself spoke of the *future* fulfilment of this prophecy. Christ said that it would be fulfilled in the day of His second coming, when He would appear in the glory of the Father. Jesus completes His statement about these signs in the heavens with the following words:

> And they shall see the Son of man coming in the clouds of heaven with power and great glory.[5]

Then Christ refers again to that hour, saying:

> When the Son of man shall come in his glory . . . before him shall be gathered all nations.[6]

Bahá'u'lláh clearly explains these, and similar passages in the Bible. He points out that all of them are symbolical truths. Such statements use *outward symbols* to illustrate *inward truths.* Specifically,

105

Baháʼuʼlláh writes:

> The term "heaven" denoteth loftiness and exaltation, inasmuch as it is the seat of the revelation of those Manifestations of Holiness [Moses, Jesus, and the other Messengers] . . . though delivered from the womb of their mother, [they] have in reality descended from the *heaven* of the Will of God. Though they be dwelling on this earth, yet their true habitations are the retreats of glory in the realms above. Whilst walking amongst mortals, they soar in the *heaven* of the divine presence.[7]

Baháʼuʼlláh also explains the meaning of the "clouds" in which these Messengers appear:

> By the term "clouds" is meant those things that are contrary to the ways and desires of men . . . These "clouds" signify, in one sense, the annulment of laws, the abrogation of former Dispensations [teachings], the repeal of rituals and customs current amongst men, the exalting of the illiterate faithful above the learned opposers of the Faith. In another sense, they mean the appearance of that immortal Beauty [the Prophet] in the image of mortal man, with such human limitations as eating and drinking, poverty and riches, glory and abasement, sleeping and waking, and such other things as cast doubt in the minds of men, and cause them to turn away. All such veils are symbolically referred to as "clouds".[8]

Baháʼuʼlláh adds:

> These are the "clouds" that cause the heavens of the knowledge and understanding of all that dwell on earth to be cloven asunder . . . Even as the clouds prevent the eyes of men from beholding the sun, so do these things hinder the souls of men from recognizing the light of the divine Luminary [or Messenger of God].[9]

106

The people reject the Messenger because of these "clouds", and angrily they speak words such as these, from sacred Scripture:

> Unless an angel be sent down and take part in His warnings, we will not believe.

Bahá'u'lláh points out that all of the Prophets have been subjected to poverty and affliction, to hunger, to the ills and chances of this world. Because they were subject to such needs and wants, the people could not believe that they were Messengers of God. Consequently the people were filled with misgivings and doubts. These doubts are the "clouds", Bahá'u'lláh says, which obscure the "heaven" of their understanding.

In His *Book of Certitude,* Bahá'u'lláh explains in detail the meaning of the prophecies concerning the sun, moon, stars, and the heavens. He shows that these likewise are not to be taken in the literal sense. The Messengers of God, He says, were primarily concerned with spiritual, not material things, and with spiritual and not physical light.

When the Prophets mention the sun, in connection with the so-called Day of Judgment, they refer to the Sun of Righteousness. The star we call the sun is the supreme source of light to our physical world. In like manner, the Messenger of God is the supreme source of our spiritual light. Moses was the sun of the Jews, Christ the sun of the Christians, Muhammad the sun of the Muslims, and Bahá'u'lláh the sun of the Bahá'ís.

When the Prophet speaks of the sun being darkened, He means that the pure teachings of these spiritual Suns (former Messengers of God) have become obscured by misrepresentation, misunderstanding, compromise, and prejudice. The people are left in spiritual darkness because this sun no longer shines.

The moon and the stars are the lesser sources of illumination in this physical world. Hence they are used as symbols representing the religious leaders and teachers who, although lesser lights than their Prophet, still should guide and inspire the people.

When it is said that *the moon shall not give her light,* or that *it shall be turned into blood,* and *the stars fall from heaven,* it means that the leaders of religion shall become more interested in material than in spiritual things. They shall become debased. They shall engage in strife and contention. The priests and clergy shall become worldly-minded. They shall be concerned about *earthly* rather than *heavenly* things. Therefore, these moons and stars are darkened and shed no light. Their thoughts are turned toward flesh and blood instead of toward the spirit. They value the lamp itself more than they do the light within it.

The moon has no light of its own. It receives its light from the sun. The moon shines with this reflected light after the disappearance of the sun. In similar manner, these religious leaders, the disciples and followers of the Prophet, receive their light from this Messenger of God. They are the moons of His Sun; they reflect His light upon the world after He has departed. Their brightness is not that of the Sun. It is a lesser, reflected light, but it comes from the same, one original Sun. Thus when the Messenger has left the earth, these religious leaders (moons) brighten the heavens of man's understanding which would be dark without them. These religious leaders are also the lesser lights of night, the stars. They do not have the brightness of the sun, but men can chart their course by these stars when the sun of day has disappeared.

Bahá'u'lláh, writing to the religious leaders of Christianity, declared:

Ye are the stars of the heaven of My knowledge. My mercy desireth not that ye should fall upon the earth.[10]

The meaning of such prophecies is of course not exhausted by one explanation. There are other ways in which these symbols can be interpreted. Bahá'u'lláh tells us that in yet another sense, the words "sun" and "moon" and "stars" are applied to the laws, ordinances and instructions which are given by the Messenger of God

Each Messenger of God changes the forms, rituals, and customs of the former Messenger. He alters them according to the needs of the age in which He appears. Enactments such as marriage, divorce, prayer, baptism, etc. are changed or modified by each new Messenger of God. So, in this sense, Bahá'u'lláh says, the "sun" and "moon" are changed, and the "stars" are scattered and dispersed. These laws and instructions fall from their place of honour. They no longer shed light upon man's problems in a more advanced age. Therefore, they disappear and fade from sight with the appearance of the new Sun of Truth, or Messenger of God; just as the moon and stars vanish when the physical sun appears above the horizon.

In His own words, Bahá'u'lláh says:

> It is evident and manifest unto every discerning observer that even as the light of the star fadeth before the effulgent splendour of the sun, so doth the luminary of earthly knowledge, of wisdom, and understanding vanish into nothingness when brought face to face with the resplendent glories of the Sun of Truth [Messenger of God], the Day-star of divine enlightenment.[11]

The moon has no light of its own. It receives its light from the sun. If it were possible for the moon to refuse the light of the sun, which is the sole source of its illumination, it would become a dark, dead sphere. The moon must take its light from the sun. When the sun of yesterday is gone, it must take its light from the sun of today.

Therefore, the prophecies say, when the moon (or religious leaders) refuse to recognize the new Sun (or Messenger) it will no longer give off light. It cannot shed light upon the people if it has turned away from the source of its light. Such a moon (religious leader) is no longer spiritual since it has lost its light. It is wholly material. It is of the "flesh" not the "spirit", and therefore it is said that it has "turned into blood".

In another way, just as clouds obscure the sun, so do clouds hide the moon. When dust storms arise, the sun appears red. On certain occasions in history these dust clouds in the sky have turned the moon an awesome red. The "clouds" of doubt or misunderstanding which cover the Sun of Truth, and surround the moons of His teaching, turn the *moon into blood,* just as the clouds of the earth turn the physical moon red.

In many cases, the literal fulfilment of these prophecies would of course be impossible and contrary to reason. The Bahá'í teachings declare:

> Whatever the intelligence of man cannot understand, religion ought not to accept. Religion and science walk hand in hand, and any religion contrary to science is not the truth.[12]

For example, it would be absurd for the moon to be literally turned into blood. It would serve no purpose. It would be physically impossible for the stars to fall on the earth. Even the remote approach of a star would consume the earth. The smallest of the visible stars is immeasurably greater than the earth. It would be as though the "greatest of all mountains were to fall upon the tiniest mustard seed". It is an utter impossibility.

There are other "signs in the heavens" mentioned in the holy Books. *Matthew* relates that Christ said:

> And he shall send his angels with a great sound of a trumpet, and they shall gather together his elect from the four winds, from one end of heaven to the other.[13]

The appearance of "angels" accompanying the promised Messiah is spoken of in other places in the Bible as well as in other holy Books.

Bahá'u'lláh writes of this, saying:

> And now, concerning His words: "And He shall send His angels . . ." By "angels" is meant those who, reinforced by the power of the spirit, have consumed, with the fire of the love of God, all human traits and limitations, and have clothed themselves with the attributes of the most exalted Beings . . . inasmuch as these holy beings . . . have become endowed with the attributes of the spiritual, and have been adorned with the

110

noble traits of the blessed, they therefore have been designated as "angels".[14]

Those selfless and devoted souls who believe in God and His Messenger, and who dedicate their lives to serving their fellow men and in spreading the word of God are "angels". Such receptive souls will indeed hear the sound of His "trumpet" and will respond to the call "from the four winds, and from one end of heaven to the other". For this "trumpet" is the voice of the Messenger of God. His teachings are the sound of the trumpet which both attracts and alarms humanity.

In the same chapter in which *Joel* says, the "sun and the moon shall be dark, and the stars shall withdraw their shining", he also associates the "trumpet" with the day of the coming of the Messiah. He declares:

> Blow ye the trumpet in Zion . . . for the day of the Lord cometh . . .[15]

Bahá'u'lláh sounded the "trumpet" of His teachings from Zion. From this "nest of the Prophets", Israel, which is the World Centre of the Bahá'í Faith, Bahá'u'lláh's explanations revealing the inner meanings of the holy Books have gone out to the four corners of the earth. These teachings have been well received and deeply appreciated by many modern thinkers in every part of the world. An entire book has been compiled of the tributes which such world figures have paid to the greatness of the Bahá'í Faith.

Isaiah also speaks of this voice of the Messenger of God from Israel in the last days, Who will sound His "trumpet". Because of His teachings, *Isaiah* promises the people:

> . . . thy darkness (shall) be as the noonday:[16]

Isaiah prophesies that this Wondrous Personage will:

> Cry aloud, spare not, lift up thy voice like a trumpet, and shew

my people their transgression . . .[17]

If the people will hear the sound of the trumpet, if they will believe and obey, *Isaiah* promises them that:

> . . . the Lord shall guide thee continually, and satisfy thy soul in drought. . . and thou shalt be like a watered garden. . . [18]

Where before they had been in darkness, *Isaiah* says they would now be in light:

> Then shall thy light break forth as the morning, and thine health shall spring forth speedily: and thy righteousness shall go before thee . . .[19]

And most amazing of all, in this same chapter, *Isaiah* prophesies for this "believing" people:

> . . . *the glory of the Lord* shall be thy rereward.[20]

Bahá'u'lláh, Whose name means *the Glory of the Lord,* lifted up His voice, like a trumpet, in the Holy Land; from there His teachings are spreading to the whole world.

These are some of the meanings of "angels" and "trumpets" which are seen and heard in the "heaven" of man's understanding.

The followers of Moses did not understand the inner meaning of these signs and words; therefore they rejected Christ. The followers of Jesus do not understand the inner meaning of these signs and words in this day. Thus they have deprived themselves of the joy of knowing and believing in Bahá'u'lláh, Who has fulfilled all of the signs for which they are waiting, and for which they have already waited for such a long, long time.

Bahá'u'lláh writes:

> The people have always busied themselves with such specious discourses, vainly protesting: "Wherefore hath not this or that

sign appeared?" Such ills befell them only because they have clung to the ways of the divines [religious leaders] of the age in which they lived, and blindly imitated them in accepting or denying . . .'[21]

He adds:

These leaders . . . As they have literally interpreted the Word of God, and the sayings and traditions of the Letters of Unity [the Messengers], and expounded them according to their own deficient understanding, they have therefore deprived themselves and all their people of the bountiful showers of the grace and mercies of God.[22]

Bahá'u'lláh exposes the futility of an *outward* fulfilment of these prophecies, and shows how useless they would be in helping to develop the moral character of mankind. In His *Book of Certitude,* He writes:

They have even failed to perceive that were the signs of the Manifestation of God in every age to appear in the visible realm in accordance with the text of established traditions, none could possibly deny or turn away, nor would the blessed be distinguished from the miserable, and the transgressor from the God-fearing. Judge fairly: Were the prophecies recorded in the Gospel to be literally fulfilled; were Jesus, Son of Mary, accompanied by angels, to descend from the visible heaven upon the clouds; who would dare to disbelieve, who would dare to reject the truth, and wax disdainful? Nay, such consternation would immediately seize all the dwellers of the earth that no soul would feel able to utter a word, much less to reject or accept the truth.[23]

If these prophecies were to be literally fulfilled, one of the primary purposes of religion, and of the coming of the Messengers of God, would be subverted. Bahá'u'lláh warns mankind:

Know verily that the purpose underlying all these symbolic terms and abstruse allusions, which emanate from the Revealers of God's holy Cause, hath been to test and prove the peoples of the world; that thereby the earth of the pure and illuminated hearts may be known from the perishable and barren soil. From time immemorial such hath been the way of God amidst His creatures, and to this testify the records of the sacred books.[24]

Bahá'u'lláh and Christ both denounced the religious leaders of Their day, because these leaders not only denied the Messenger themselves, but they deliberately prevented their followers from understanding and accepting Him. Christ knew only too well that the religious leaders of His day refused to understand the *inward truth* behind His symbolic words. He said:

Woe unto you, lawyers! for ye have taken away the key of knowledge; ye entered not in yourselves, and them that were entering in ye hindered.[25]

Bahá'u'lláh said:

As the adherents of Jesus have never understood the hidden meaning of these words, and as the signs which they and the leaders of their Faith have expected have failed to appear, they therefore refused to acknowledge, even until now, the truth of those Manifestations of Holiness [Messengers] that have since the days of Jesus been made manifest. They have thus deprived themselves of the outpourings of God's holy grace, and of the wonders of His divine utterance.[26]

Then He warns:

O heedless people! Ye repeat what your fathers, in a bygone age, have said. Whatever fruits they have gathered from the tree of their faithlessness, the same shall ye gather also . . . [27]

Bahá'u'lláh, speaking with the same authority with which Moses and Jesus spoke of old, cries out against this spiritual blindness:

> Even as the people of Israel, in the time of Moses, bartered away the bread of heaven for the sordid things of the earth, these people, likewise, sought to exchange the divinely-revealed verses for their foul, their vile, and idle desires. In like manner, thou beholdest in this day that although spiritual sustenance hath descended from the heaven of divine mercy, and been showered from the clouds of His loving-kindness . . . yet these people, ravenous as the dogs, have gathered around carrion, and contented themselves with the stagnant waters of a briny lake. Gracious God! how strange the way of this people! . . . They scoffed at the verses, a single letter of which is greater than the creation of heavens and earth, and which quickeneth the dead in the valley of self and desire with the spirit of faith; and clamoured saying: "Cause our fathers to speed out of their sepulchres." Such was the perversity and pride of that people.[28]

This has been the story of religion in every age. The people cling tenaciously to the *outward symbols*, neglecting, forgetting, or denying the *inward truths*.

Bahá'u'lláh exclaims:

> Great God! . . . They confidently assert that such traditions as indicate the advent of the expected [Promised One] have not yet been fulfilled, whilst they themselves have failed to inhale the fragrance of the meaning of these traditions, and are still oblivious of the fact that all the signs foretold have come to pass, that the way of God's holy Cause hath been revealed, and the concourse of the faithful, swift as lightning, are even now, passing upon that way, whilst these foolish divines [religious leaders] wait expecting to witness the signs foretold. Say, O ye foolish ones! Wait ye even as those before you are waiting![29]

Thus Bahá'u'lláh has *unsealed* the meaning of the darkening of the sun and the moon, of the stars falling from heaven, of the appearance of angels, and of the sound of the trumpet. Bahá'u'lláh has disclosed the division, unhappiness, and suffering that come from looking with the *outer* and not the *inner* eye upon these truths. When the *new day* dawns, it is futile to cling to the light of yesterday, which has vanished.

The snob appeal of following the traditional and popular way has long been used to attract material-minded man. Almost everyone wants to belong to the oldest, the richest, or the most exclusive of whatever it is. Anything that is for the common man, the masses, or for everyone, is both unwelcome and unwanted. This has been true in the beginning days of every religion. Belief in the new Faith was never popular. The followers of Krishna, Moses, Zoroaster, Buddha, Christ, Muhammad, and Bahá'u'lláh were all déclassé in the early days. Immediately after the founding of their Faith they were ridiculed as a strange minority believing in some weird cult. A few examples will make this clear.

The religious leaders said to Muhammad's followers that no one followed Muhammad "except the abject amongst us, those who are worthy of no attention". To Muhammad they said, "We see not any who have followed Thee except our meanest ones of hasty Judgment."[30]

The religious leaders said almost exactly the same thing to the followers of Christ:

> Are ye also deceived?
>   Have any of the rulers or of the Pharisees believed on him?
>   But this people [followers of Jesus] who knoweth not the law are cursed.[31]

Christ made it plain that it was the purity of a man's heart, the sincerity of his belief, and not his station in life or his adherence to the old traditional path, which was important. Christ answered these same religious leaders, saying:

116

Verily I say unto you, That the publicans and the harlots go into the kingdom of God before you . . . the publicans and the harlots believed him:[32]

When Bahá'u'lláh, His family, and His followers were exiled to the great and dreadful prison of 'Akká because of His teachings, He wrote of the religious leaders of Islám:

And if anyone ask them: "For what crime were they imprisoned?" They would answer and say: "They, verily, sought to supplant the Faith with a new religion." If that which is ancient be what ye prefer, wherefore, then, have ye discarded that which hath been set down in the Torah [Old Testament] and the Evangel [New Testament]? Clear it up, O men! By My life! There is no place for you to flee to in this day. If this be My crime, then Muhammad, the Apostle of God, committed it before Me, and before Him He Who was the Spirit of God [Jesus Christ], and yet earlier He Who conversed with God [Moses]. And if My sin be this, that I have exalted the Word of God and revealed His Cause, then indeed am I the greatest of sinners! Such a sin I will not barter for the kingdoms of earth and heaven.[33]

Ezekiel prophesied of this new day in which the Word of God would be spoken to a people who would be "impudent and hard-hearted". He made it plain that men in that day would have to have inner vision in order to understand the Word of God. *Ezekiel* records:

I will open thy mouth, and thou shall say unto them, Thus saith the Lord God; . . .[34]

Then he adds:

He that heareth, let him hear . . .[35]

In this same chapter, *Ezekiel* speaks of the wonder of this vision, and of beholding *the glory of the Lord.* He says:

> . . . and, behold, *the glory of the Lord* stood there, as the glory which I saw by the river of *Chebar:* and I fell on my face.[36]

The river Chebar, known of old as the river Khabar, has its source west of Baghdad and empties into the Euphrates in ancient Babylon. It was in this very region, near the Chebar, that Bahá'u'lláh, Whose name means *the Glory of the Lord,* announced His Mission. In this same region Bahá'u'lláh revealed His *Kitáb-i-Íqán* (*Book of Certitude*) which has been quoted so frequently in this volume. It has been written of this Book of Bahá'u'lláh's,

> . . . it proffered to mankind the "Choice Sealed Wine", whose seal is of "musk", and broke the "seals" of the "Book" referred to by Daniel, and disclosed the meaning of the "words" destined to remain "closed up" till the "time of the end".[37]

It was in this book, the *Book of Certitude,* that Bahá'u'lláh clearly and beautifully explained the meaning of all those things which have puzzled and divided men in the past. In this book, Bahá'u'lláh *unsealed* the secrets of both the Old and the New Testament, and laid bare the "gems of Truth" which were concealed there.

CHAPTER TWELVE

THE MEANING OF RESURRECTION

What is the meaning of the *Resurrection* of His Holiness Jesus the Christ? It is written that after three days He rose from the dead. How can this be explained to the logical mind?

Bahá'u'lláh has also *unsealed* the meaning of the "resurrection" of Christ and the meaning of "resurrection day". Bahá'u'lláh pointed out that there was a beautiful, eternal truth hidden in this *inward symbol* of the *Resurrection,* but that it had been gravely misunderstood. As a result, it became the cause of disputes between religions, as well as between religion and science. The doctrine of the Resurrection has also been the cause of preventing literal-minded people from accepting the new Messenger of God, Bahá'u'lláh, in this day.

By clinging to this belief in the bodily resurrection, the eyes of the people have become blinded to the truth. They have deprived themselves of the *spiritual resurrection,* the very basic purpose of their existence on earth. Such people are truly "dead" in the "graves" of error.

The teachings of the Bahá'í Faith say:

The *resurrections* of the [Messengers of God] are not of the body . . . Their parables, and Their instructions have a spiritual and divine signification, and have no connection with material things.[1]

In the Gospel of *John* it says:

And no man hath ascended *up* to heaven, but he that came *down* from heaven, even the Son of man which is *in* heaven.[2]

Again in *John* it is written:

For I came down from heaven . . .[3]

Christ says in these verses that He, the Son of man, is in heaven at the time while He, Christ, *is on earth.* He also says that he came down from heaven, though physically it is known that He came from the womb of Mary and that His physical body was born of Mary.

Is it any wonder that the people could not understand these verses? We can appreciate their bewilderment, as expressed in *John*:

And they said, Is not this Jesus, the son of Joseph, whose father and mother we know? how is it then that he saith, I came down from heaven?[4]

There can be no doubt that when it is said: the Son of man is "come down from heaven", this is a spiritual truth, not a material fact. It means that although Christ was, apparently, born from the womb of Mary, His spirit, and the reality of His teachings, came from God.

Just as Christ's *coming down from heaven* is a spiritual rather than a physical fact, so too His *disappearance* under the earth for three days, His subsequent *resurrection* and ascension up to heaven are spiritual, not physical facts. They are all *inward,* not *outward* truths.

Bahá'u'lláh's teachings say clearly:

Therefore we say that the meaning of Christ's *resurrection* is as follows: The disciples were troubled and agitated after the martyrdom of Christ. The *Reality of Christ,* which signifies His teachings, His bounties, His perfections and His spiritual power, was hidden and concealed for two or three days after His martyrdom, and was not resplendent and manifest. No, rather it was lost; for the believers were few in number and were troubled and agitated. The Cause of Christ was like a lifeless body; and, when after three days the disciples became assured and steadfast, and began to serve the Cause of Christ, and resolved to spread the divine teachings, putting His counsels into practice, and arising to serve Him, the *Reality of Christ* became resplendent and His bounty appeared; His religion found life; His teachings and His admonitions became evident and visible. In other words, the Cause of Christ was like a lifeless body until the life and bounty of the Holy Spirit surrounded it.[5]

Let us examine the *inner meaning* of the *resurrection* and, by means of the Scriptures, prove to our own satisfaction that it *is* symbolical.

The *resurrection* and *ascension* of Christ, if taken literally, are contrary to science and to reason. Bahá'u'lláh's teachings say that any religion which is contrary to true science is nothing more than superstition.

Science has proved that there are stars in space millions of light years away from us. If the physical body of Christ were to ascend into a heaven beyond this universe, the journey would not be completed yet. It would take millions of years, and He would still be ascending. Mathematicians, during the 1840s, scoffed at those literal-minded Bible scholars who said Christ would soon appear "on a cloud". Clouds, they said, are vapours which rise from the earth, they do not "come down". They also pointed out that Christ would have to make hundreds of thousands of "solo flights" if all the world were to see Him, because of the curvature of the earth.*

Obviously, the *coming*, the *resurrection*, and the *ascension* of Christ were symbolical.

---

* See *Thief in the Night*, pp. 1–5.

If Christ really had risen physically from the dead, then all His patient love and teaching would be fruitless. Men would believe in Him solely because of this miracle, and not because of a sincere, voluntary effort on their part to turn toward God. A miracle of this nature would compel the wickedest sinner to repent. The *sheep* and the *goats* would both respond to the force of this prodigy, and moral values would be set aside. Belief would be brought about by coercion. This is contrary to the spirit of the teachings of Christ, as well as to those of all the Messengers of God.

Furthermore, if Christ's greatness were to be based on His physical *ascent* into heaven, then Elijah would have an equal claim to that station of greatness. It is written in the Old Testament that many years before Christ Elijah ascended into heaven with his physical body. In the *Second Book of Kings* it is recorded:

> And it came to pass, as they still went on, and talked, that, behold, there appeared a chariot of fire, and horses of fire, and parted them both [Elijah and Elisha] asunder; and *Elijah went up by a whirlwind into heaven.*[6]

Enoch would also have an equal station, for he, too, as is related in both *Genesis* and *Hebrews,* was taken up by God with his physical body "that he should not see death".

Durant, in *Caesar and Christ,* writes that the idea of such a translation "into the sky in body and in life was familiar to the Jews; they tell it of Moses, Enoch, Elijah and Isaiah."[7]

Such an ascent is also described before the time of Christ, concerning Mithra, of whom it is said, ". . . in the end, his earthly mission fulfilled, Mithra after a Last Supper ascended into heaven, where he has never ceased to succour his own."[8]

Clearly these *ascents,* including that of Christ, are to be understood symbolically.

If Christ's greatness were based upon His resurrection from the tomb with a physical body, then there are many saints who should be considered equally as great, for they, too, were resurrected by God. It is recorded that they came out of their graves with their physical bodies, just as Christ had done. Perhaps their resurrection is even more meritorious, since they were *resurrected* not three days after their deaths, but after far longer periods of time.

It is written in *Matthew* that Christ gave up the ghost:

> And the graves were opened; and many bodies of the saints which slept arose,
>> And came out of the graves after his resurrection . . .[9]

If the greatness of Christ is based upon the fact that He not only arose from the dead, but proved it to His followers by appearing to them, then these saints must still be considered equally great, for they, too, not only resurrected, but also proved it by appearing to many. It is written in *Matthew* that they:

> . . . came out of the graves after his resurrection . . . *and appeared unto many.*[10]

Obviously, these words are meant to be taken symbolically, not literally.

There is scarcely a person who does not believe that the story of Jonah, who was three days and three nights in the belly of the whale, has an inward symbolical meaning rather than an outward physical one. That the *resurrection* of Christ is in like manner to be taken symbolically is shown by His own words. Christ likens His own death, and burial, to that very story of Jonah and the big fish.

When the Pharisees accused Christ of casting out devils with the help of the prince of devils, Beelzebub, Jesus branded those who believed such a doctrine a "generation of vipers". They asked Christ for a *sign*. They wanted a *proof* or a *miracle* to show that He was the Messiah.

> Then certain of the scribes and of the Pharisees answered, saying, Master, we would see a *sign* from thee.[11]

Christ refused to work a miracle or to give them a sign. He said:

> An evil and adulterous generation seeketh after a *sign;* and there shall no sign be given to it, but the sign of the prophet Jonas:
>
> For as Jonas was three days and three nights in the whale's belly; so shall the Son of man be three days and three nights in the heart of the earth.[12]

Christ was crucified on the day which has come among Christians to be known as Good Friday. He arose, or was resurrected, from the earth on what is called Easter Sunday. Obviously He was then only *two* nights, Friday night and Saturday night, in the earth and not *three* nights as Christ promised He would be. The meaning is obviously a symbolical one.

Jonah was chosen by God to go to Nineveh and cry against that wicked city. Jonah did not wish to go. He was reluctant to carry out his responsibility. He fled from the face of the Lord. The spirit died within him, and he was cast into the *sea of materialism.* He was swallowed up by the *whale of earthly desires and disobedience.* All signs of Jonah's spiritual life had vanished. Jonah himself declared that he cried out to the Lord from "hell". The belly of the whale was the grave of his disobedience and lack of understanding.

At last, obedient to the edict of Almighty God, Jonah turned his heart to Nineveh and to his responsibilities. The *whale* and the *sea* gave up their treasure, for Jonah's spirit could no longer be restrained by such graves. He was resurrected. He went to Nineveh. He was afire with the miracle of the rebirth which God had caused in his soul. He preached to the wicked city of Nineveh. The people repented, and they were saved through the *resurrection* of Jonah.

In a like manner, it was not the body of Christ, but the body of His Cause, His teachings, which were buried in the earth, in the grave of neglect. When His disciples, under the inspiration of a woman, Mary of Magdala, realized in their hearts that Christ was with them always in spirit and that His preaching and teaching were the source of all life, then the *body of Christ's Faith* was *resurrected.*

George Townshend, sometime Canon of St Patrick's Cathedral, in Dublin, Ireland, and Archdeacon of Clonfert has expressed this in his book *The Heart of the Gospel.* He writes of the disciples and their earnest belief, to the very last moment, that Christ's kingdom was to be an earthly one in which they would enjoy positions of glory and power among men.

> The tragic close of His [Christ's] career brought their spiritual failure to unmistakable expression. Peter denied His Master thrice; Thomas doubted Him; Judas betrayed Him; all in the hour of His danger forsook Him and fled. The crucifixion cast them into utter amazement and despair . . . Their world was empty. Their beloved Lord was defeated – the mocking Scribe was right. They had made some terrible mistake. . . *For three days the Cause of Christ lay in their hearts dead and buried.* None can tell what might have happened, had it not been for the intuition and courage of one who was not of their number – a woman, Mary of Magdala. She it was who was the first to understand the reality of eternal life and Christ's eternal Sonship . . . and recognized that if His body was dead, His spirit was indestructible and was alive breathing in mortal power. She cheered the disciples. She communicated to them her vision, quickened their faith and renewed their courage.[13]

Thus, after three days, the Body of Christ's teachings was *resurrected,* and it arose from that tomb of death.

The symbolical use of death in this sense is frequent and unmistakable throughout the Bible. For example we find in the New Testament:

> And you hath he quickened who were *dead* in trespasses and sins;[14]

And again:

But she that liveth in pleasure [sins of the flesh] is *dead* while she liveth.[15]

Bishop E. W. Barnes quotes the early Christian work, the *Shepherd of Hermas*, as saying: "Those who are baptized descend into the water dead, and they rise alive."

And in another place the New Testament declares:

For as the *body* without the spirit is *dead,* so *faith* without works is *dead* also.[16]

The *Body* of Christ's Faith, without the works of His disciples to give it life, was *dead* for three days.

Bahá'u'lláh comments with sadness upon the failure of mankind to grasp the meaning of such Scriptural events as the *resurrection.*

Again and again they read those verses which clearly testify to the reality of these holy themes, and bear witness to the truth of the Manifestations [Messengers] of eternal Glory, and still apprehend not their purpose. They have even failed to realize, all this time, that, in every age, the reading of the scriptures and holy books is for no other purpose except to enable the reader to apprehend their meaning and unravel their innermost mysteries. Otherwise reading, without understanding, is of no abiding profit unto man.[17]

Unless the Scribes, the Pharisees, and the people of this day believed in the *resurrection* and life which the *Word* of Christ could give them, they would be spiritually dead. This was the sign of Jonah and the sign of Christ. It was an *outward symbol* of the *inward truth.*

Christ, in His very last words on earth, at the crucifixion, emphasized this principle once again:

And when Jesus had cried with a loud voice, he said, Father, into thy hands I commend my spirit . . .[18]

His *spirit,* not his *body.* Christ was eager for His disciples to under-stand the meaning of His words. He told them:

> It is the *spirit* that quickeneth; the *flesh* profiteth nothing: the *words* that I speak unto you, *they* are spirit, and *they* are life.[19]

Christ demonstrated that it was the preaching, the words which He spoke, that the people must pay attention to if they were to have life. These words, this preaching, was the sign of Jonah. This was the miracle which Christ promised to give them. He said:

> The men of Nineveh shall rise in judgment with this generation, and shall condemn it: because *they repented at the preaching of Jonas;* and, behold, a greater than Jonas is here.[20]

Paul's first epistle to the Corinthians also shows plainly the sym-bology of the *resurrection.* He says of this inward truth:

> So also is the *resurrection* of the dead. It is sown in corruption; it is raised in incorruption . . . It is sown a natural body; it is raised a spiritual body . . . this mortal must put on immortality.[21]

In the same chapter, Paul says of the resurrection of Christ:

> . . . he was seen of James; then of all the apostles. And last of all he was seen of me also . . .[22]

Now Christ's appearances to His disciples after the resurrection took place long before Paul's experience on the road to Damascus. Dunkerly, in *Beyond the Gospels,* says, ". . . it is interesting to find Paul speaking of his conversion as one of the resurrection appear-ances; this raises problems as to the nature of the resurrection, but we cannot enter into that here."[23]

In one of the famous creeds of the Christian church are found the words: "He descended into Hell, the third day He rose again from the dead." It is further stated in this creed that true faith is based upon the belief in the "resurrection of the body".

As shown in the chapter on Heaven and Hell, these are not *places,* with a *devil* in charge of evil at one end, and a *God* in charge of *good at* the other. This would be a duality of authority, and would mean that the oneness and infinity of God would be destroyed. This would be contrary to science and reason. It is necessary to understand these truths symbolically.

Man's failure to understand that these truths are figurative, and his rigid insistence upon their literal interpretation, have led to the weakening and discrediting of religion. To maintain that the resurrection of Christ was unique and solely a miracle of Christ, leads to grave problems, for we shall see that the symbol of the bodily resurrection is not limited to Jesus and to Christianity. Although Alexander Cruden, in his unabridged Concordance of the Bible, stated that, "The resurrection is a doctrine unknown to the wisest heathens, and peculiar to the gospel," we find that similar[24] phenomena have been attributed to many gods in the Mediterranean area. Some of these resurrection stories date back to nearly 3,000 years before Christ. These tales of the death and *resurrection* of the gods were commonly known, until they were suppressed by force in the fourth century of the Christian era.

Among the gods who performed this miracle of death and resurrection were: Mithra, Dionysus, Osiris, Attis, Persephone, Eurydice, and Aphrodite. The Feast of Saturnalia in which a mock king is slain as an atoning sacrifice for the people was one of the most thoroughly enjoyed spectacles.

Patterson, in his *Mithraism and Christianity,* and Smith, in his *Man and His Gods,* both speak of the outward similarity in these resurrection stories. Toynbee lists "eighty-seven correspondences between the story of Jesus' life and the stories of certain Hellenic 'saviours' . . ." Adonis was buried in a stone tomb. He was mourned; then he was declared resurrected, following which he ascended into heaven.[25]

The demi-god Herakles in myth was sent by God to maintain a kingly authority over mankind. He suffered agonies. He resigned himself to the will of his heavenly father. He was sacrificed, and his mortal remains miraculously disappeared. He descended into hell. He made special appearances to the women of his gatherings. The death and glorious resurrection of Herakles were celebrated each year in a festival at Tarsus, the boyhood home of Paul.[26]

As the similarity between Christian rituals and those of other beliefs becomes more generally known, it is obvious that an insistence on a literal acceptance of such truths as the resurrection can only lead to the gradual weakening and dissolution of the faith of the individual Christian. Whereas an understanding of the symbolic nature of these truths, and of their true meaning, can only serve to fortify and strengthen his belief.

Taken as a literal truth, *resurrection* can only serve to divide and separate. Taken symbolically, it tells the simple, beautiful story of the continual *death* and *rebirth* of the spirit, a process very similar to the *death* of the earth in winter and its *rebirth* in the springtime.

When the Christians preach the truth of Christ crucified, it is the *inward symbol* of His sacrifice that is important, not the *outward fact* that He was crucified. Christ's greatness does not depend upon His crucifixion, for He shares this distinction with thousands and thousands of others, many criminals of the worst sort. Crucifixion was not a unique punishment given only to Jesus. The Roman highways, in those days, were dotted with punished criminals who had been crucified. It was the most commonly accepted form of punishing serious offenders. It is interesting to note that some sources state that a tree and not a cross was used for such punishment. Victims of crucifixion were hanged or nailed to a tree, or a pole, with their hands above their heads. When the Galileans followed Judas the Gaulonite as the Messiah, during the rule of the procurator Quirinius, two thousand of them were crucified in one mass slaughter.

Throughout the lives of these World Educators, or Messengers of God, it is always the spirit which is important, never the body.

One of the strongest and clearest proofs which Christ gave to prove that bodily resurrection was useless in changing the hearts of men can be found in the Gospel of *Luke*. Jesus wanted to make certain once and for all that everyone understood this point: that it was the *Message of the Prophets* which was important, and which brought new life, not a miracle such as resurrection.

In His parable of Lazarus and the rich man, Christ declares that *even the miracle of physical resurrection* will not aid those who lack the capacity to hear and to follow the Messengers of God.

The rich man from the depths of hell called upon Father Abraham to send a special messenger to his five brothers; lest, because of their disobedience to the laws of God, they too might be cast into hell.

Abraham replied:

They have Moses and the prophets; let them hear them.

The rich man, according to this parable given by Christ, implored for something greater than words or teachings. He wanted a *sign,* a *miracle* to awaken his brothers. He said:

Nay, father Abraham: but *if one went unto them from the dead, they will repent.*

The answer, for all time, is recorded in Abraham's reply:

If they hear not Moses and the prophets, *neither will they be persuaded, though one rose from the dead.*[27]

There could be no clearer statement of the unimportance of the physical return from the grave. Nor could there be stronger emphasis upon the importance of the words and teachings of the Messengers of God. This parable is from the words and teachings of Christ Himself upon the unimportance of resurrecting from the dead. He stressed that the *spirit* which the Prophets bring through their teachings can do more to aid humanity than any such outwardly astounding signs as "raising from the dead".

The terms "life" and "death", Bahá'u'lláh tells us, refer to the "life" of faith and the "death" of unbelief. It is the spirit of faith and belief which brings about the resurrection. Just as we say that in the winter the world is dead, and remains so until the springtime comes to awaken and revive it. This, also, is resurrection.

The dead will speed out of their sepulchres in the last day, according to Scripture. Again, this is a spiritual truth, Bahá'u'lláh tells us. It means that when the Prophet or Messenger of God appears, it is the Day of Judgment for all. It is *the last days* of the old religion. A new spiritual springtime has come. The spiritually dead will be awakened and will speed out of their sepulchres of unbelief. Their physical bodies do not come back from physical graves. Never!

The physical body is of little importance other than as a channel or instrument for the ever-developing spiritual qualities within man. Christ Himself told the young man who wanted to delay his acceptance of Jesus long enough to bury his father: ". . . let the dead bury their dead. . . ."[28] He meant, let those who do not believe (i.e. the spiritually dead), bury the physically dead. In another place He says: "The flesh profiteth nothing" and "that which is born of the flesh is flesh; and that which is born of the Spirit is spirit".[29]

Bahá'u'lláh writes:

In every age and century, the purpose of the Prophets of God and their chosen ones hath been no other but to affirm the spiritual significance of the terms "life", "resurrection", and "judgment" . . . Wert thou to attain to but a dewdrop of the crystal waters of divine knowledge, thou wouldst readily realize that true life is not the life of the flesh but the life of the spirit. For the life of the flesh is common to both men and animals, whereas the life of the spirit is possessed only by the pure in heart who have quaffed from the ocean of faith and partaken of the fruit of certitude. This life knoweth no death, and this existence is crowned by immortality. Even as it hath been said: "He who is a true believer liveth both in this world and in the world to come." If by "life" be meant this earthly life, it is evident that death must needs overtake it.[30]

According to Bahá'u'lláh's teachings, resurrection is the birth of the individual into spiritual life. It comes through the gift of the Holy

Spirit bestowed upon man by Christ and the other Messengers of God in whatever age they may appear. The grave from which the individual arises is the *grave* of ignorance and negligence of God. The *sleep* from which he awakens is the dormant spiritual condition in which many await the dawn of the new Day of God. This dawn, or coming of the Messenger of God, illuminates all who live on the face of the earth. Everyone, except those who are spiritually blind, will see and recognize it.

The present Day of Resurrection is not a day of twenty-four hours, but an era which has already begun. It will last as long as men are being called from their graves of spiritual death or lack of faith and belief. The Messenger of God for this day, Bahá'u'lláh, is calling upon all men to arise from their graves of doubt and error, just as Christ called to them in the reign of the Roman Caesars.

This is the true meaning behind "being born again". From spiritual death man is brought to spiritual life. Jesus said: "Ye must be born again." Whoever was quickened by His Word attained to new life and to resurrection. It is the same in this day. Bahá'u'lláh has breathed the Words of God upon humanity, and all those who are quickened by this life-giving spirit, attain to the Day of Resurrection and are thus delivered from the graves of spiritual death.

There is a verse concerning this truth in the sacred Scriptures of Islám, which says:

> When the Qa'im (Promised One) riseth that day is the Day of Resurrection.[31]

This is the day when new "life" has been bestowed upon man by God's Messenger; therefore, man has been rescued from "death". Bahá'u'lláh says:

> . . . the people, owing to their failure to grasp the meaning of these words, rejected and despised the person of the Manifestation [Messenger of God], deprived themselves of the light of His divine guidance, and refused to follow the example of that immortal Beauty.[32]

The teachings of Bahá'u'lláh's Faith state that resurrection has "nothing to do with the gross physical body. That body, once dead, is done with. It becomes decomposed and its atoms will never be recomposed into the same body."[33]

Jesus knew that His spirit would return, when bidden by God, in another human temple (flesh). Otherwise He would not have repeatedly warned His followers to watch and be alert for the time of His return. There would have been no need to warn them if He, Christ, were literally and physically to "return" in the clouds with "angels".

There is yet one final consideration. Suppose Christ were to descend to the earth in the flesh, what then? Who would be able to recognize Him? Even our artists have painted Him after their own imaginations. Sometimes He has fair skin, sometimes dark. Some picture Him with blue eyes and some with black; with blonde hair or brunette; slight or sturdy. After nearly two thousand years, who could possibly recognize Him? If we say, "God would assist us to recognize Him," then let us remember the following remarkable facts:

A. (*John* 20:14–15) It is less than three days since the crucifixion of Christ. Yet, Mary Magdalene does not know Christ when He appears to her. It is not 2,000 years but less than 72 hours.

> . . . she turned herself back, and saw Jesus standing, and knew not that it was Jesus. Jesus saith unto her, Woman, why weepest thou? whom seekest thou? She, supposing him to be the gardener, saith unto him, Sir, if thou hast borne Him hence, tell me where thou hast laid him, and I will take him away.

Mary Magdalene, from whom Jesus had cast seven devils. Mary Magdalene, who had kept the vigil through the hour of the agony on the cross, did not recognize Christ until He called to her and said, "Mary".

What chance would strangers have nearly twenty centuries later?

B. *(John 21:4)* A few days later, Jesus appeared to His disciples. He was close enough to converse with them. In spite of this, they failed to recognize Him.

> But when the morning was now come, Jesus stood on the shore: but the disciples knew not that it was Jesus.

Not until Christ had filled their net with a multitude of fish. Not until He performed a miracle, did they know it was He, Jesus. These were His chosen disciples, but a few hours after His crucifixion.

C. *(Matthew 28:16–17)* Jesus made an appointment with His disciples in Galilee after His death. "There they shall see me," He promised:

> Then the eleven disciples went away into Galilee, into a mountain where Jesus had appointed them.
> And when they saw him, they worshipped him: but some doubted.

Even of the chosen eleven, *some doubted;* although they were awaiting Jesus by appointment.

D. *(Luke 24:36–37)*

> Jesus himself stood in the midst of them, and saith unto them, Peace be unto you. But *they were terrified and affrighted, and supposed that they had seen a spirit.*

They didn't know Him though he stood in their midst.

E. *(Luke 24:15–16)*:

> . . . while they communed together and reasoned, Jesus himself drew near, and went with them. But their eyes were holden that they should not know him.

They called Jesus "stranger" until He made Himself known unto them.

In every case, Christ made Himself known to His closest chosen disciples by words, by miracles, or by an example. They did not know Him by their outward sight.

Now, nearly 2,000 years later, how could His followers, divided into hundreds of sects, hating each other, devoid of the closeness, dedication and intimacy which Christ's disciples enjoyed, ever hope to recognize Him in the flesh? The answer is simple: they could not.

The teachings of the Bahá'í Faith also liken resurrection, or the coming of a Messenger of God such as Christ or Bahá'u'lláh, to a *spiritual springtime*. In the world of nature, the Spring not only brings about the growth and awakening of new life, but also causes the destruction of the old and effete. The same sun that makes flowers grow and trees bud also brings about the decay and disintegration of what is dead and useless. The Spring loosens the ice and melts the snow of Winter. It sets in motion the flood and the storm which cleanse and purify the earth. Following this, new life is born on all sides. Every man glories in the beautiful and fragrant resurrection of life in the Springtime after the cold Winter of a dead and frozen world.

This same process takes place in the world of man's spirit. The spiritual springtime caused by the coming of a Messenger of God brings about similar commotion and change. Thus, the Day of Resurrection is also the Day of Judgment. The Day in which corruption and imitation of truth are discarded. Outworn ideas and customs that no longer fit the age are done away with. The ice of prejudice and the snow of superstition, which accumulated during the Winter of religious decline are melted and transformed. Spiritual energies which have been frozen up are released to flood and renovate the world. Things that were dead come to life again in this spiritual springtime. The fruits, vegetables, and grains come to life in this new physical springtime so that man can be fed and nourished. In like manner, the spiritual springtime of the coming of the Prophet brings the spiritual foods without which mankind would wither away and die spiritually. If it were not for this spiritual resurrection, man would remain dead, buried in the grave of his animal nature.

In Bahá'u'lláh's words, *resurrection, rebirth,* and *return* all have the same fundamental meaning: the spiritually dead are *resurrected* from their graves of heedlessness. Those who have passed into spiritual death while living, are *reborn.* Those qualities of love, integrity, and justice, which have vanished from men's lives, *return* with the coming of God's Messenger.

Each Prophet comes from the same single heaven of the knowledge of an Infinite and Almighty God. Each brings the same light of truth to a darkened world. Hence, they are called Suns. The sun is the source of the light of day. *Resurrection* comes from the Latin word *sugere,* "to rise", with the prefix "re" meaning *again.* To rise again. When the Sun of Truth, the Messenger of God, rises again on a night of earthly darkness, He brings the *Day of Resurrection.* This is the *Day of God that* "rises again" and renews all things.

It is also the *Day of Judgment.* On the Day when the Messenger of God appears, all are judged by their acceptance or rejection of His Message. The sheep are separated from the goats by His appearance. The sheep recognize the voice of the Good Shepherd, and follow Him, "for they know his voice".[34]

Bahá'u'lláh writes:

> Behold how the generality of mankind hath been endued with the capacity to hearken unto God's most exalted Word – the Word upon which must depend the gathering together and spiritual *resurrection* of all men . . .[35]

From the preceding explanations, we can be sure that the resurrection of Christ is to be understood symbolically. It is plainly an *inward truth:* the body of Christ's Faith was dead. It *arose* again with its real life of the spirit. The *outward symbol* of this *inward truth* is the story of the *Resurrection.*

Bahá'u'lláh has *unsealed* this spiritual or inner meaning and made it crystal clear in His Writings. The *outward symbol* is this: the body of Christ rose from the dead. The *inward truth* is this:

the body of His Faith was dead because of the fear and the scattering of His followers. Through the courage and determination of His disciples it rose from this state of apparent extinction and appeared with its real life, that of the Spirit. It was *resurrected*.

This is the true meaning of resurrection.

Bahá'u'lláh says:

> The mysteries of Resurrection and the events of the Last Hour are openly manifest, but the people are sunk in heedlessness and have suffered themselves to be wrapt in veils.[36]

In another place, Bahá'u'lláh declares that it was for the purpose of helping mankind to understand this truth that He *unsealed,* in detail, the meanings from the sacred Books:

> O brother, behold how the inner mysteries of "rebirth", of "return", and of "resurrection" have each, through these all-sufficing, these unanswerable, and conclusive utterances, been unveiled and unravelled before thine eyes. God grant that through His gracious and invisible assistance, thou mayest divest thy body and soul of the old garment, and array thyself with the new and imperishable attire.[37]

The explanation of other puzzles, such as the story of *Adam and Eve,* the story of *Creation,* the *immortality of the soul, free-will, reincarnation,* and *proofs of the existence of God,* have been explained elsewhere.

The present book has dealt only with basic Christian subjects.

Ninety years ago hardly anyone would teach the Christian Bible in Persia. Bahá'u'lláh asked, "Why?"

He was told, "It is not the Word of God."

Bahá'u'lláh replied, "You must read it with an understanding of its meaning, not as those who merely recite words."

Now, Bahá'ís all over the world read and study the Bible. They love and revere Moses and Christ. They spread the truth of this Holy Book everywhere.

Bahá'u'lláh has opened the eyes of the entire world to the beautiful teachings to be found in the sacred Books of the Christians and Jews. He has spread the Cause of Christ in the heart of Islám, Hinduism, Zoroastrianism, and Buddhism. He has made these teachings understandable and acceptable to the scientist and the skeptic. He has removed "the barriers of names".[38]

Thus, Bahá'u'lláh has fulfilled completely the prophecy from the Book of Psalms which gave this volume its title. He has, indeed, *unsealed* "the wine of astonishment" so that the beloved of God might drink and be "delivered" from the superstitions of the past. Bahá'u'lláh has cleared away the misunderstandings and doubts which were caused by literal interpretations, and has clarified the meaning of the sacred Scriptures of all Religions.

If you believe the things you have read in this book, you are now faced with one of the most important decisions of your life. If you feel that Bahá'u'lláh has *unsealed* the sacred Books and brought you a richer understanding of their truth, then this is still one more proof that He is the *Promised One* of all religions. For this reason you owe it to yourself and to your fellowmen to investigate the Bahá'í Faith with all the ardour and thoroughness at your command.

The Bahá'í Faith offers a single powerful answer to the problems that beset our present-day civilization. The Writings of Bahá'u'lláh's Faith clearly demonstrate that there is one basic underlying cause for all these modern tragedies: man is out of touch with God and with the world of spiritual values. Man is still more material than he is moral or spiritual. He should be both, in balance. Since man ignores these basic spiritual and moral values, he finds himself in his present dilemma of war crime, delinquency, mental illness, divorce, alcoholism, and the other heart-breaking evidences of his own spiritual immaturity. In the Bahá'í Faith you will find the remedy for these ills. What's more, you will find that the remedy works. This is not a vague and pious hope; it is a promise.

The Bahá'í Faith has demonstrated its power to unite people of every national background, every colour of skin, every level of society, and every religious origin. In every part of the world the

Bahá'ís are doing something about their Faith – not just talking about it. Because of this spirit of enthusiasm, the Bahá'í Faith has been described as the most "rapidly growing" world Faith in religious history.

If you find the Word of Bahá'u'lláh to be the truth, as I am confident you will, then arise and serve it. This is the finest way in which you can serve your fellow man today. Upon such action may depend not only your own peace of mind and tranquillity, but the well-being, security, and future happiness of all mankind. Ask yourself this question: are the following words written about Bahá'u'lláh true?

> The mysteries of the Holy Books have become explained in the manifestation of Bahá'u'lláh. Before He appeared these mysteries were not understood. Bahá'u'lláh opened and *unsealed* these mysteries.[39]

The final decision rests with you.

NOTE ONE

For a more thorough and more beautiful explanation of the relationship of Christianity to the Bahá'í Faith, read *Some Answered Questions, Paris Talks,* and *The Promulgation of Universal Peace,* by 'Abdu'l-Bahá, the son of Bahá'u'lláh.

The views set forth in the preceding chapters are limited by my own background as a Christian. I was searching for a greater truth which I felt might be more suited to the present day. Therefore, much of the accent in this present volume is on the Christian viewpoint. In the works of 'Abdu'l-Bahá you will receive a pure, crystal stream of knowledge and wisdom, exceedingly refreshing and full of exciting new horizons applicable to all religions.

The famous Orientalist and scholar, Edward Granville Browne of Cambridge University, who met and talked with 'Abdu'l-Bahá, praised His depth of knowledge of the sacred Scriptures. Browne wrote:

> Subsequent conversation with him ['Abdu'l-Bahá] served only to heighten the respect with which his appearance had from the first inspired me. One more eloquent of speech, more ready of argument, more apt of illustration, more intimately acquainted with the sacred books of the Jews, the Christians, and the Muhammadans, could, I should think, scarcely be found. . . . These qualities, combined with a bearing at once majestic and genial, made me cease to wonder at the influence and esteem which he enjoyed even beyond the circle of

his father's followers. About the greatness of this man and his power no one who had seen him could entertain a doubt.[1]

Herbert Putnam, Librarian of the American Congress at the time of 'Abdu'l-Bahá's visit to America in 1912, wrote:

A personality combining a dignity so impressive, with human traits so engaging. I wish that he could be multiplied.[2]

Professor Yone Noguchi was deeply moved by the explanations which 'Abdu'l-Bahá gave to all the difficult questions which were presented to Him for answer. He said,

His ['Abdu'l-Bahá's] words are as simple as the sunlight; again like the sunlight, they are universal. . . . No teacher, I think, is more important today than 'Abdu'l-Bahá.[3]

Canon T. K. Cheyne, Bible scholar and famous Christian clergyman, called 'Abdu'l-Bahá an "Ambassador to humanity".

NOTE TWO

The Bahá'í Faith offers a wonderful ethical and moral code for the development of the individual. It also establishes fundamental principles for a world-wide social plan which can rehabilitate the human race.

These principles have already been tested on a planetary scale in some eight thousand centres in every continent and in the islands of the seas, under the direction of the World Centre of the Faith which is in Haifa–'Akká, Israel, the Holy Land. Fifty-six National and Regional Assemblies, freely elected by the adult Bahá'ís of the world, represent over 258 major countries, sovereignties, and dependencies.*

The Bahá'í Faith has raised Houses of Worship in the Americas, in Europe, in Asia, in Australia, and in Africa: Houses of Worship dedicated to the oneness of all religions.

The number of Bahá'ís has doubled and trebled throughout the world during the past few years. Figures as to numbers given one year become obsolete the next, so rapidly is this World Faith capturing the hearts of the peoples of the world, among men and women and children of every skin colour and belief.

Among the basic principles proclaimed by Bahá'u'lláh to establish peace and order in the world in this day, are the following:

---

* The growth of the Bahá'í community is strikingly demonstrated by a comparison of the statistics on the previous page and on p. 137, as cited by the author in 1963, with those for 2004: nearly 102,000 centres throughout the world, with 183 National Spiritual Assemblies, and 9,631 local Assemblies. (Ed.)

1. The oneness of mankind.
2. Independent investigation of truth.
3. The common foundation of all religions.
4. The essential harmony of science and religion.
5. Equality of men and women.
6. Elimination of prejudice of all kinds.
7. Universal compulsory education.
8. A spiritual solution of the economic problem healing the social relationships of nations.
9. A universal auxiliary language.
10. Universal peace upheld by a world government.

Bahá'u'lláh has brought not only the principles, but the laws, agencies, and institutions to establish and maintain an enduring peace among all nations. This system is based upon universal representation, and an unquestioned belief in the oneness of God, His Messengers, and the entire human race.

NOTE THREE

The name *Bahá'u'lláh,* when translated into English, means *the Glory of God.* The name *Christ,* when translated into English, means *the Anointed.*

Jesus of Nazareth was the name of the Founder of Christianity. He was known by the title *Christ.* Husayn-'Alí of Núr was the name of the Founder of the Bahá'í Faith. He was known by the title *Bahá'u'lláh.*

Bahá'u'lláh was also known as Bahá (Glory). A person who believes in Him was, therefore, known as a Bahá'í. Bahá(í) means *of Bahá'u'lláh.** Christ(ian) means *of Christ.*

A Christian is a follower of Christ, and a Bahá'í is a follower of Bahá'u'lláh.

It is that simple.

The Bahá'í Faith began in Persia (Iran) in 1844. Bahá'u'lláh, the Founder, is a descendant of Abraham, whose "seed" would "inherit the earth" in the last days.†

---

* Bahá'í is pronounced: Ba-ha'-ee
  Bahá'u'lláh is pronounced: Ba-há'-ol-láh.
† The astonishing story of how Bahá'u'lláh was driven in exile from Persia to the Holy Land, fulfilling prophecy after prophecy from the Bible and holy Books of other religions, is told in detail in *Thief in the Night,* by the same author.

BIBLIOGRAPHY

'Abdu'l-Bahá. *Paris Talks.* London: Bahá'í Publishing Trust, 1967.

— *The Promulgation of Universal Peace.* Wilmette, IL: Bahá'í Publishing Trust, 1982.

— *Some Answered Questions.* Wilmette, IL: Bahá'í Publishing Trust, 1994.

Bahá'í World Faith. Wilmette, IL: Bahá'í Publishing Trust, 2nd edn. 1976.

Bahá'u'lláh. *Epistle to the Son of the Wolf.* Translated by Shoghi Effendi. Wilmette, IL: Bahá'í Publishing Trust, rev. edn. 1976.

— *Gleanings from the Writings of Bahá'u'lláh.* Translated by Shoghi Effendi. Wilmette, IL: Bahá'í Publishing Trust, rev. edn. 1978.

— *The Kitáb-i-Íqán. The Book of Certitude.* Translated by Shoghi Effendi. Wilmette, IL: Bahá'í Publishing Trust, 6th edn. 1974; London: Bahá'í Publishing Trust, rev. edn. 1978.

— *The Summons of the Lord of Hosts.* Haifa: Bahá'í World Centre, 2002.

— *Tablets of Bahá'u'lláh Revealed After the Kitáb-i-Aqdas.* Wilmette, IL: Bahá'í Publishing Trust, 1988.

Barnes, Ernest William. *The Rise of Christianity.* London: Longmans, Green & Co, 1947.

Baudouin, Charles, Eden Paul and Cedar Paul. *Contemporary Studies.* Part III. Allen & Unwin, 1924. RP Books for Libraries Press, 1969.

Cruden, Alexander. *Cruden's Complete Concordance to the Bible.* London: Lutterworth Press, rev. edn 1977.

Dhalla, Maneckji Nusservanji. *Zoroastrian Theology: From The Earliest Times To The Present Day.* New York, 1914. RP Bombay 1999.

Dunkerley, Roderic. *Beyond the Gospels.* London: Penguin 1961.

Durant, Will. *The Story of Civilization* (1935–75). Vol. III: *Caesar and Christ*; Vol. IV: *The Age of Faith*. New York: Simon & Schuster, 1944, 1950.

Gibbon, Edward. *Decline and Fall of the Roman Empire* (1776–89). Ed. David Womersley. London: Allen Lane, 1994. New York: Penguin, 2005.

Patterson, L. *Mithraism and Christianity: A Study in Comparative Religion*. London: Cambridge University Press, 1921.

Rowley, Harold Henry. *The Unity of the Bible*. London: Varey Kingsgate Press, 1953.

Sears, William. *Thief in the Night*. Oxford: George Ronald, 1961, 2007.

Shoghi Effendi. *The Advent of Divine Justice*. Wilmette, IL: Bahá'í Publishing Trust, 1971.

— *God Passes By*. Wilmette, IL: Bahá'í Publishing Trust, 1979.

— *The Promised Day is Come*. Wilmette, IL: Bahá'í Publishing Trust, rev. edn. 1980.

Smith, Homer William. *Man and His Gods*. New York: Grosset and Dunlap, 1956.

Strachey, Marjorie. *The Fathers Without Theology. The Lives and Legends of the Early Church Fathers*. New York: George Braziller, 1958.

Taylor, I. *The Medieval Mind: A History of the Development of Thought and Emotion in the Middle Ages*. Harvard: Harvard University Press, 1951.

Townshend, George. *The Heart of the Gospel*. Oxford: George Ronald, 1960, 1995.

Toynbee, Arnold. *A Study in History*. New York: Oxford University Press, 1950.

Wells, H. G. *The Outline of History*. New York: Garden City Publisher, 1925.

REFERENCES AND NOTES

Chapter One: The Seals Are Opened
1. Sears, *Thief in the Night*, pp. 152–3.
2. *Habakkuk* 1:5.
3. ibid. 2:14.
4. Sears, *Thief in the Night*, pp. 175–6.
5. *Enoch* 46:2.
6. *Isaiah* 29:18, 24.
7. *I Corinthians* 4:5.

Chapter Two: Out of the Sea of Knowledge
1. *Isaiah* 29:11.
2. ibid. 29:18, 24.
3. ibid. 35:1–2.
4. *Daniel* 12:9.
5. ibid. 7:9–10.
6. *Revelation* 22:10.
7. ibid. 14:14.
8. ibid. 5:9.
9. ibid. 21:23.

Chapter Three: How to Unravel the Secret of the Scriptures
1. Baudouin, *Contemporary Studies*, Part III, pp. 139–46.
2. 'Abdu'l-Bahá, *Some Answered Questions*, p. 83.
3. ibid.
4. Shoghi Effendi, *The Advent of Divine Justice*, p. 66.
5. Bahá'u'lláh, *Gleanings*, pp. 281–2.

Chapter Four: The Meaning Behind the Ritual of Baptism
1. *Jeremiah* 2:13.
2. *Revelation* 7:17.
3. *Isaiah* 58:11.
4. ibid. 58:8–9.

5. *Habakkuk* 2:14.
6. ibid. 1:5.
7. *John* 3:5.
8. ibid. 3:3.
9. Barnes, *The Rise of Christianity*, p. 277.
10. Durant, *The Age of Faith*, p. 528.
11. ibid.
12. Barnes, *The Rise of Christianity*, p. 280.
13. *Mark* 16:16.
14. *Matthew* 28:19.
15. *I Corinthians* 1:17.
16. *Acts* 18:8.
17. ibid. 2:38.
18. ibid. 2:41.
19. ibid. 8:12.
20. ibid. 8:13.
21. *Shepherd of Hermas*, Similitude ix, 16.
22. Barnes, *The Rise of Christianity*, p. 259.
23. *Acts* 8:36-8.
24. *Luke* 23:43.
25. ibid. 7:50.
26. ibid. 3:16.
27. Rowley, *The Unity of the Bible*, p. 155.
28. *Matthew* 7:21.
29. *Acts* 15:1.
30. *I Corinthians* 7:18-19.
31. *Colossians*, 2:11.
32. Bahá'u'lláh, *Gleanings*, p. 11.

Chapter Five: The Bread and the Wine, Confession and Penance
1. Rowley, *The Unity of the Bible*, p. 147.
2. *John* 6:51.
3. ibid. 6:54.
4. ibid. 6:63.
5. *I Corinthians* 10:2-3.
6. *John* 6:35.
7. 'Abdu'l-Bahá, *Some Answered Questions*, Part 2; xxi.
8. *John* 7:37-8.
9. ibid. 7:39.
10. ibid. 4:31-4.
11. Durant, *Caesar and Christ*, p. 600.
12. ibid. p. 599.
13. ibid. pp. 599-600.

14. Barnes, *The Rise of Christianity*, p. 295.
15. Rowley, *The Unity of the Bible*, p. 155.
16. ibid. p. 142.
17. Barnes, *The Rise of Christianity*, p. 280.
18. Durant, *The Age of Faith*, pp. 740–1.
19. Taylor, *Medieval Mind*, I, p. 551.
20. Durant, *The Age of Faith*, pp. 591–2.
21. ibid. p. 740.
22. ibid.
23. Townshend, *Heart of the Gospel*, p. 136.
24. Bahá'u'lláh, *Tablets of Bahá'u'lláh*, p. 24.
25. Durant, *Caesar and Christ*, p. 616.
26. *Matthew* 26:26–8.
27. 'Abdu'l-Bahá, *Some Answered Questions*, Part 2:xxi.
28. *John* 6:27.
29. ibid. 6:28–9.
30. *I Corinthians* 15:50.
31. *John* 6:48, 50, 55.
32. ibid. 6:60–3.
33. ibid. 6:66.
34. Smith, *Man and His Gods*, p. 201.
35. Bahá'u'lláh, *Gleanings*, pp. 175–6.
36. ibid. p. 176.

Chapter Six: The Meaning of: Jesus, Son of God

1. Durant, *Caesar and Christ*, p. 601.
2. 'Abdu'l-Bahá, *Some Answered Questions*, Part 2:xviii.
3. *John* 14:7–9.
4. ibid. 14:10.
5. ibid. 14:26.
6. ibid. 8:57–9.
7. *The Song of God: Bhagavad-Gita*, p. 133.
8. Exodus 3:14-15
9. *Matthew* 19:17.
10. Bahá'u'lláh, *Gleanings*, p. 102.
11. Bahá'u'lláh, *Kitáb-i-Íqán*, pp. 120–1.
12. *John* 10:30.
13. ibid. 10:31–3.
14. ibid. 10:34–9.
15. ibid. 5:19.
16. ibid. 12:49.
17. Bahá'u'lláh, *Kitáb-i-Íqán*, p. 182.
18. *John* 5:39, 40, 43.

19. Bahá'u'lláh, *Kitáb-i-Íqán*, p. 182.
20. *John* 5:45–7.
21. *Hebrews* 7:3.
22. *Luke* 3:38.
23. *John* 1:12.
24. *Psalms* 82: 1, 6.
25. ibid. 82:6.
26. *I John* 3:1.
27. *Revelation* 21:7.
28. 'Abdu'l-Bahá, *Some Answered Questions*, Part 2:xii.
29. Bahá'u'lláh, *Kitáb-i-Íqán*, p. 134.

Chapter Seven: In the Glory of the Father

1. *John* 10:16.
2. *Ezekiel* 34:13.
3. ibid. 34:23, 25.
4. *Isaiah* 40:10–11.
5. ibid. 40:5.
6. *Micah* 7:12.
7. ibid. 7:14.
8. ibid. 7:15.
9. *Isaiah* 35:2.
10. ibid. 35:5.
11. Bahá'u'lláh, *The Summons of the Lord of Hosts*, p. 86.
12. *Mark* 12:1–9.
13. Bahá'u'lláh, *Gleanings*, pp. 162, 163.
14. Nategh, *Religious Debates*, p. 30.
15. Dhalla, *Zoroastrian Theology*, p. 182.
16. ibid. p. 181.
17. ibid. p. 182.
18. Cited Durant, *Age of Faith*.
19. Dhalla, *Zoroastrian Theology*, p. 60.
20. ibid. p. 61.
21. Shoghi Effendi, *God Passes By*, p. 94.
22. Shoghi Effendi, *The Promised Day is Come*, p. 31.
23. ibid. pp. 104–5.
24. ibid. p. 106.
25. ibid. p. 106.
26. *John* 16:7.
27. ibid. 16:23.
28. ibid. 16:25.
29. ibid. 16:13, 15.
30. Shoghi Effendi, *The Promised Day is Come*, pp. 26–7.

31. ibid. p. 27.
32. ibid. pp. 109–110.
33. ibid. p. 110.

Chapter Eight: The Secret of the Trinity
1. Gibbon, *Decline and Fall of the Roman Empire*, III, p. 75.
2. Smith, *Man and His Gods*, p. 227.
3. Wells, *Outline of History*, p. 545.
4. *John* 1:1–2.
5. Strachey, *Fathers Without Theology*, p. 48.
6. ibid. p. 107.
7. Durant, *Caesar and Christ*, p. 660.
8. Smith, *Man and His Gods*, p. 224.
9. Durant, *Age of Faith*, p. 8.
10. *John* 16:13, 15.
11. Shoghi Effendi, *God Passes By*, p. 101.
12. Bahá'u'lláh, *Gleanings*, pp. 166–7.
13. 'Abdu'l-Bahá, *Some Answered Questions*, Part 2:xxvii.
14. ibid.
15. Smith, *Man and His Gods*, p. 210.
16. Durant, *Age of Faith*, p. 484.
17. *Bahá'í World Faith*, p. 191.

Chapter Nine: Miracles
1. *Luke* 17:17–18.
2. *John* 20:29.
3. ibid. 12:37.
4. 'Abdu'l-Bahá, *Some Answered Questions*, Part 2:ix.
5. Shoghi Effendi, *Advent of Divine Justice*, pp. 21–2.
6. ibid.
7. 'Abdu'l-Bahá, *Promulgation of Universal Peace*, p. 364.
8. *John* 3:12.
9. Bahá'u'lláh, *Gleanings*, pp. 94–6.
10. *Judges*, 6:13.
11. Durant, *Age of Faith*, pp. 984–5.
12. ibid. p. 985.
13. ibid.
14. Shoghi Effendi, *God Passes By*, p. 144.
15. Bahá'u'lláh, *Gleanings*, p. 132.
16. Shoghi Effendi, *God Passes By*, p. 144.
17. ibid. p. 144; *Some Answered Questions*, Part 1:ix.
18. Bahá'u'lláh, *Gleanings*, p. 132.
19. *John* 6:26.

20. 'Abdu'l-Bahá, *Some Answered Questions*, Chap. XXII.
21. Smith, *Man and His Gods*, p. 130.
22. Durant, *Caesar and Christ*, p. 617.
23. Smith, *Man and His Gods*, p. 202.
24. Bahá'u'lláh, *Gleanings*, p. 86.
25. Bahá'u'lláh, *Epistle to the Son of the Wolf*, p. 33.
26. Bahá'u'lláh, *Gleanings*, p. 200.

Chapter Ten: Heaven and Hell – Not a Matter of Geography

1. Esslemont, *Bahá'u'lláh and the New Era*, p. 204.
2. *Cruden's Concordance* (see 'hell').
3. *Psalms* 55:15.
4. *Jonah* 2:2.
5. *Revelation* 19:13.
6. ibid. 20:13.
7. ibid. 21:23.
8. 'Abdu'l-Bahá, *Promulgation of Universal Peace*, p. 90.
9. ibid.
10. *Bahá'í World Faith*, p. 145.

Chapter Eleven: When the Stars Fell From Heaven

1. Bahá'u'lláh, *Kitáb-i-Íqán*, p. 28.
2. ibid. p. 28.
3. *Joel* 2:31; 3:1–2; 2:10.
4. *Matthew* 24:29–30.
5. ibid. 24:30.
6. ibid. 25:31–2.
7. Bahá'u'lláh, *Kitáb-i-Íqán*, p. 67.
8. ibid. pp. 71–2.
9. ibid. p. 72.
10. Shoghi Effendi, *Promised Day Is Come*, p. 101.
11. Bahá'u'lláh, *Kitáb-i-Íqán*, p. 37.
12. 'Abdu'l-Bahá, *Paris Talks*, p. 131.
13. *Matthew* 24:31.
14. Bahá'u'lláh, *Kitáb-i-Íqán*, pp. 78–80.
15. *Joel* 2:1.
16. *Isaiah* 58:10.
17. ibid. 58:1.
18. ibid. 58:11.
19. ibid. 58:8.
20. ibid.
21. Bahá'u'lláh, *Kitáb-i-Íqán*, pp. 81–2.
22. ibid. p. 82.

23. ibid. pp. 80–1.
24. ibid. p. 49.
25. *Luke* 11:52.
26. Bahá'u'lláh, *Kitáb-i-Íqán*, p. 80.
27. ibid. p. 207.
28. ibid. pp. 208–9.
29. ibid. p. 83.
30. ibid. p. 222.
31. *John* 7:47–9.
32. *Matthew* 21:31–2.
33. Bahá'u'lláh, *Epistle to the Son of the Wolf*, p. 52.
34. *Ezekiel* 3:27.
35. ibid.
36. ibid. 3:23.
37. Shoghi Effendi, *God Passes By*, p. 139.

Chapter Twelve: The Meaning of Resurrection

1. 'Abdu'l-Bahá, *Some Answered Questions*, Part 2:xxiii.
2. *John* 3:13.
3. ibid. 6:38.
4. ibid. 6:42.
5. 'Abdu'l-Bahá, *Some Answered Questions*, Part 2:xxiii.
6. *II Kings* 2:11.
7. Durant, *Caesar and Christ*, pp. 573–4.
8. Barnes, *The Rise of Christianity*, p. 59.
9. *Matthew* 27:52–3.
10. ibid. 27:53.
11. ibid. 12:38.
12. ibid. 12:39–40.
13. Townshend, *Heart of the Gospel*, pp. 132–3.
14. *Ephesians* 2:1.
15. *I Timothy* 5:6.
16. *James* 2:26.
17. Bahá'u'lláh, *Kitáb-i-Íqán*, p. 172.
18. *Luke* 23:46.
19. *John* 6:63.
20. *Matthew* 12:41.
21. *I Corinthians* 15:2, 44, 53.
22. ibid. 15:7–8.
23. Dunkerley, *Beyond the Gospels*, p. 19.
24. *Cruden's Concordance* (see "resurrection", early edition only).
25. Smith, *Man and His Gods*, pp. 187, 181, 182.
26. ibid. p. 182.

27. *Luke* 16:29–31.
28. *Matthew* 8:22.
29. *John* 3:6.
30. Bahá'u'lláh, *Kitáb-i-Íqán*, p. 120.
31. ibid. p. 144.
32. ibid. p. 114.
33. Esslemont, *Bahá'u'lláh and The New Era,* pp. 239–40.
34. *John* 10:4.
35. Bahá'u'lláh, *Gleanings,* p. 97.
36. Bahá'u'lláh, *Tablets of Bahá'u'lláh,* pp. 40–1.
37. Bahá'u'lláh, *Kitáb-i-Íqán,* p. 158.
38. See 'Abdu'l-Bahá, *Promulgation of Universal Peace,* p. 212.
39. ibid. p. 197.

APPENDIX Note One:
1. Introduction, *Episode of The Báb,* E. G. Browne, pp. 35–6.
2. Appreciations of the Bahá'í Faith.
3. ibid. pp. 59–60.